Contents

Introduction 2

Unit 1: Tools of Physical Science
Background Information 3
Review 10
Units of Measurement 12
Converting Units 13
Scientific Notation 14
Significant Figures 15
Taking Measurements 16
Working with Equations 18
Vectors 19
Tools of Physical Science Crossword 20

Unit 2: Motion
Background Information 21
Review 25
Speed and Velocity 26
Graphing Speed 27
Acceleration 28
Speed and Acceleration Graphs 29
Projectile Motion 30
Centripetal Acceleration 31
Motion Word Find 32

Unit 3: Force
Background Information 33
Review 41
Newton's Second Law 43
Newton's Third Law 44
Momentum and Impulse 45
Force Diagrams 46
Mass and Weight 47
Forces in Orbital Motion 49
Density 50
Buoyancy 51
Friction 52
Force Crossword 53

Unit 4: Energy
Background Information 54
Review 60
Kinetic Energy 62
Gravitational Potential Energy 63

Work 64
Conservation of Energy in a
    Simple Pendulum 65
Power 67
Simple Machines 68
Mechanical Advantage 70
Efficiency 71
Energy Word Find 72

Unit 5: Heat
Background Information 73
Review 79
Temperature Conversions 81
Conduction, Convection, and Radiation 82
Specific Heat 83
Latent Heat and Phase Changes 84
Heat Engines 85
Heat Crossword 86

Unit 6: Waves
Background Information 87
Review 93
Transverse and Longitudinal Waves 94
Frequency, Period, Wavelength, and
    Wave Speed 95
The Electromagnetic Spectrum 96
The Law of Reflection 97
Refraction and Snell's Law 98
Waves Word Find 99

Unit 7: Electricity and Magnetism
Background Information 100
Review 108
Electric Charge and Electric Force 109
Potential Difference, Current, and
    Resistance 110
Series and Parallel Circuits 111
Electric Power 112
The Magnetic Field Around a Wire 113
Charges Moving in Magnetic Fields 114
Electricity and Magnetism Crossword 115

Glossary 116

Answer Key 117

Contents
Physical Science, SV 0425-5

Introduction

This book is designed to serve a variety of needs and interests for teachers, students, parents, and tutors. The contents of this book are based upon both state and national standards. Teachers can use this book for review and remediation. Students will find the content to be concise and focused on the major concepts of the discipline. Parents can use this book to help their children with topics that may be posing a problem in the classroom. Tutors can use the material as a basis for their lessons and for assigning problems and questions.

Each unit follows the same sequence in covering a major topic. Each unit opens with *Key Terms*, which include all the boldfaced terms and their definitions presented in the same order as they are introduced in the text. As a result, the reader can develop a sense of the topics that are covered in the unit. The unit follows with a clear and concisely written text, which is divided into several sections. Each section is written so that the reader is not overwhelmed with details but rather guided through the topic in a logical sequence. Each unit then moves on to a *Review*, which consists of several multiple-choice and short-answer questions. The questions follow the same sequence as the material presented in the unit. As a result, the reader can easily locate the section where a review may be needed. Each unit concludes with a series of *activities*. These activities are designed to assess the reader's understanding of the content and to apply the information learned to novel situations. As a change of pace, some of the activities are meant to engage the reader in a "fun-type" exercise using a crossword puzzle or other similar device as a way of reinforcing the content. The book concludes with a *Glossary*, which lists all the boldfaced terms in alphabetical order, and an *Answer Key*, which gives the answers to all the activity questions.

This book has been designed and written so that teachers, students, parents, and tutors will all find it easy to use and follow. Most importantly, students will benefit from this book by achieving at a higher level in class and on standardized tests.

UNIT 1

Tools of Physical Science

Physical science is the study of the fundamental nature and behavior of the physical world, the world around us, the world of matter and energy. Every person is a scientist to some degree. From the time you were a child, you made observations about the world, formed ideas about how things work, and then used those ideas to predict future events. The study of physical science involves this same process.

The biggest difference between the informal science that everyone does and formal scientific study is the use of mathematics. Scientists make their ideas about the physical world more formal and precise by expressing them mathematically, in the form of equations. Scientists also take measurements of physical quantities to test their hypotheses, and use mathematical tools to analyze data.

Physical science is at the root of all other kinds of science, because everything is ultimately made of matter and follows physical laws. Many of the tools used in physical science are also used in other sciences. So learning to use the tools of physical science can help you understand not only physics and chemistry, but also biology, astronomy, geology, various applied sciences (such as medicine and engineering), and even social sciences (such as sociology and economics). Even if you don't want to be a scientist in your career, understanding the fundamentals of physical science can help you understand the advances in science and technology

Key Terms

conversion factor—a ratio between two different units of measurement that is equal to 1

scientific notation—a method of notation in which numbers have one nonzero digit to the left of the decimal point, the remaining digits to the right of the decimal point, and are multiplied by a power of ten

precision—the exactness of a measurement

accuracy—how close a measured quantity is to its actual value

significant figures—the digits in a physical quantity that are known with certainty, plus one uncertain digit

vector—a quantity that has both magnitude and direction

Unit 1, Tools of Physical Science
Physical Science, SV 0425-5

that affect the lives of everyone in modern society.

Units of Measurement

When you study mathematics, you usually use pure numbers (like 2, or 7.5, or π) or variables that represent pure numbers (such x and y). In science, however, numbers are used to represent physical quantities—quantities that correspond to something in the physical world. When you use numbers in science, it is therefore important to know what kind of quantity a number represents. This is done by specifying *units of measurement* for each quantity.

For example, if you see the quantity "3.5 m," you know that it is a measurement of distance, because meters are units of distance. If you see "3.5 m²" instead, you know that is a measurement of area. You should always remember to specify the units of measurement when you record scientific data, put numbers into scientific equations, or express scientific quantities in any other context.

In the United States and the United Kingdom, we often use units of measurement from the British/U.S. system, such as inches, feet, miles, quarts, gallons, pounds, and degrees Fahrenheit. However, many other countries around the world use different units of measurement, even in everyday life. In order to make communication between scientists around the world easier, most scientists use units of measurement from the *Système Internationale* (International System), abbreviated "SI." The table at the bottom of this page shows the SI units for several physical quantities.

Converting Units

One advantage of using SI units is that these units can use prefixes representing multiples of powers of ten. For example, "500 000 m" can also be expressed as "500 km," or "0.005 s" can be expressed as "5 ms." The table below shows the most commonly used prefixes and their corresponding powers of ten, from largest to smallest.

Powers-of-Ten Prefixes

Power	Prefix	Abbreviation
10^6	mega-	M
10^3	kilo-	k
10^{-2}	centi-	c
10^{-3}	milli-	m
10^{-6}	micro-	μ
10^{-9}	nano-	n

To convert between different units, you can multiply quantities by **conversion factors.** A conversion factor is a ratio between two different units that is equal to 1. For example:

$$\frac{1 \text{ kg}}{1000 \text{ g}} = 1 \quad \text{or} \quad \frac{10^{-9} \text{ m}}{1 \text{ nm}} = 1$$

Because conversion factors are equal to 1, multiplying a quantity by a conversion factor will not change the quantity. The number and the units will change, but the actual quantity being described is the same.

Some SI Units of Measurement

Quantity	Units	Quantity	Units
time	seconds (s)	electric charge	coulombs (C)
distance	meters (m)	current	amperes (A)
mass	kilograms (kg)	potential difference	volts (Ω)
force	newtons (N)	resistance	ohms (W)
energy	joules (J)	magnetic field strength	teslas (T)
temperature	kelvins (K)	luminous intensity	candelas (cd)

You can also use conversion factors to switch from one system of units to another, such as from the British/U.S. system to SI units. The table below shows the relationships between some common units in these two systems.

Conversions Between British/U.S. and SI Units

British/U.S. System	SI
1 in.	2.54 cm
1 ft	0.305 m
1 mi	1.61 km
1 qt	0.946 L
1 lb	4.448 N

You can also use more than one conversion factor in succession to get to the units you want. Let's look at a common example. Say you want to convert 55 miles per hour (mph or mi/h) to the SI units of meters per second (m/s). You can do this with a series of 4 conversion factors:

$$55 \frac{mi}{h} \times \frac{1.61 \text{ km}}{1 \text{ mi}} \times \frac{1000 \text{ m}}{1 \text{ km}} \times \frac{1 \text{ h}}{60 \text{ min}} \times \frac{1 \text{ min}}{60 \text{ s}} = 25 \text{ m/s}$$

Note that all the conversion factors are equal to 1. All the units on the left side of this equation cancel each other out except m in the numerator and s in the denominator, leaving the desired units of m/s on the right.

Scientific Notation

Scientific notation is another useful tool for expressing physical quantities. Numbers in scientific notation have one nonzero digit to the left of the decimal point, the remaining digits to the right of the decimal point, and are multiplied by a power of ten. Scientific calculators and many computer calculators let you enter numbers in scientific notation using a key such as "E," "EE," or "EXP" before entering the power of ten.

To convert numbers to scientific notation, remember that powers of ten correspond to moving the decimal point to the left or the right. For example, to convert the quantity 375,000 m to scientific

notation, move the decimal point to the left until there is only one nonzero number to the left of the decimal point. The number of places you moved to the left—5 in this case—is the power of ten to use:

$$375{,}000 \text{ m} = 3.75 \times 10^5 \text{ m}$$

If you move the decimal point to the right, the power of ten is negative:

$$0.00052 \text{ kg} = 5.2 \times 10^{-4} \text{ kg}$$

When multiplying quantities in scientific notation, you multiply the first part of the numbers together, then add the exponents on the powers of ten. Remember to multiply the units, too. For example:

$$(3.75 \times 10^5 \text{ m})(2.0 \times 10^2 \text{ m}) =$$

$$(3.75)(2.0) \times 10^{(5 + 2)} \text{ m}^2 = 7.5 \times 10^7 \text{ m}^2$$

When dividing quantities in scientific notation, you divide the first part of the numbers, then subtract the exponents on the powers of ten:

$$\frac{3.75 \times 10^5 \text{ m}}{2.5 \times 10^2 \text{ s}} = \left(\frac{3.75}{2.5}\right) \times 10^{(5-2)} \text{ m/s} =$$

$$1.5 \times 10^3 \text{ m/s}$$

When adding or subtracting quantities in scientific notation, the quantities must 1) use the same units and 2) have the same powers of ten. If they don't, you should convert the numbers so they do. Then you add or subtract the first part of the number, and do nothing to the power of ten. For example:

$$(3.75 \times 10^5 \text{ m}) - (2.0 \times 10^6 \text{ cm}) =$$

$$(3.75 \times 10^5 \text{ m}) - (2.0 \times 10^4 \text{ m}) =$$

$$(3.75 \times 10^5 \text{ m}) - (0.20 \times 10^5 \text{ m}) =$$

$$3.55 \times 10^5 \text{ m}$$

Using scientific notation has many advantages. It allows you to express very large or very small numbers without having long strings of zeros. It helps you to do some calculations, or at least estimates, in your head. Scientific notation also helps you to keep track of significant figures, as will be explained in the next section.

Significant Figures

Imagine that you have climbed a mountain that is reported to be 1200 m high. You then build up a pile of rocks at the summit, and you measure the height of your pile to be 1.2 m. Can you now correctly claim that the height of the mountain is 1201.2 m? No, you can't, because the reported original height was not very precise. "1200 m" could be anywhere from 1150 m to 1250 m. The 1.2 m height of your rock pile is very small compared to the uncertainty in the original height measurement.

The exactness of a measurement is called **precision**. This is not to be confused with **accuracy**, which describes how close a measured quantity is to its actual value. The precision of a physical quantity is reflected in the number of **significant figures**—the digits in a measurement that are known with certainty, plus one uncertain digit.

So how many significant figures are in the quantity "1200 m"? This is ambiguous because the last 2 numbers are zeros. The zeros could be significant, or they could just be place-holders, so "1200 m" could have 2, 3, or 4 significant figures. When faced with such ambiguity, you must assume the lowest degree of precision. So, "1200 m" has 2 significant figures. This ambiguity could be avoided by using scientific notation. "1.2×10^3 m" has 2 significant figures, while "1.200×10^3 m" has 4 significant figures.

The rules for determining whether or not zeros are significant are as follows:

- Zeros between other nonzero digits are significant.
- Zeros in front of nonzero digits are not significant.
- Zeros at the end of a number but to the left of the decimal point are not significant.
- Zeros at the end of a number and to the right of the decimal point are significant.

When multiplying or dividing physical quantities, *the result can have only as many significant figures as the measurement with the smallest number of significant figures.* Any additional digits must be rounded off. For example:

$$(3.75 \times 10^5 \text{ m})(2.3 \times 10^2 \text{ m}) = 6.3 \times 10^7 \text{ m}^2$$

Using a calculator to find this product would give you an answer of "6.325×10^7 m²." But because one of the original numbers has only 2 significant figures, the final answer can have only 2; the last of these must be rounded—in this case, rounded down—based on the following digit.

When adding or subtracting, the rule is slightly different: *the result can only be as precise as the least precise measurement.* If all the measurements have the same power of ten, then this means the result can only have as many digits to the right of the decimal point as the measurement with the smallest number of decimal places. For example, if you are subtracting 12.1 m from 15.78 m, your answer can only be precise to one-tenth of a meter because that is the precision of the quantity 12.1 m. Therefore, you must round the answer so that it has only one place to the right of the decimal point:

$$15.78 \text{ m} - 12.1 \text{ m} = 3.7 \text{ m}$$

It is important to remember that calculators don't pay attention to significant figures. It is up to you to round off answers from your calculator to give the answer the appropriate significant figures. You should also round off before starting another kind of calculation in a series, such as when switching from multiplication/division to addition/subtraction.

Taking Measurements

Collecting quantitative data is an important part of any scientific inquiry. When collecting data, it is important to understand the limitations of the instruments you are using, and to keep track of the uncertainty in your measurements.

A *digital instrument* provides a digital readout of the quantity the instrument is measuring. Examples include digital thermometers, digital voltmeters, and digital scales or balances. When using a digital instrument, you can usually assume that the last digit reported by the instrument is uncertain. Therefore, simply recording all the digits reported by the instrument ensures that you have the correct number of significant figures in your data.

An *analog instrument* reports data on a scale that depends on a physical phenomenon that is *analogous* to the physical quantity you are measuring. For example, in a mercury thermometer, the volume of the mercury in the thermometer is analogous to the temperature at the base of the thermometer. Analog instruments are *calibrated* in such a way that the scale where you read the measurement corresponds as closely as possible to the quantity you are trying to measure. A simple instrument such as a ruler can also be considered an analog instrument; the length along the ruler's scale is analogous to the length of the distance you are measuring.

When using an analog instrument, you should record as many digits as the scale of the instrument allows, plus one additional estimated digit. For example, an analog thermometer may have a scale marked to a precision of one-tenth of a degree. This allows you to be certain of the first digit to the right of the decimal point. When recording temperature data with such a thermometer, you should also estimate the next digit, so that your measurements will all have two digits to the right of the decimal point.

When you are taking measurements, you should also take care to avoid certain common errors. One such error involves *parallax*, which is an apparent shift in position caused by a change in viewing angle. One familiar example of parallax occurs when a passenger views a car's speedometer from the passenger seat. To avoid measurement errors resulting from parallax, you should always make sure your eyes are lined up with the part of the scale you are reading.

Another common error occurs when reading the volume of a liquid in a graduated cylinder. The

surface of water in a glass container tends to curve upward, as if climbing up the glass. This forms a curved *meniscus* at the surface, as shown at right. The correct way to measure volume in such a case is to take the reading at the bottom of the meniscus.

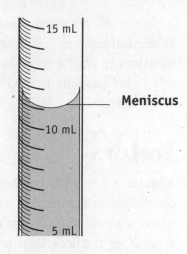

One other common error involves simply recording the wrong units of measurement. This is especially easy to do on a digital instrument that may allow you to set the instrument to read at different scales. To avoid this error, always make sure you check the scale of the instrument before recording your data.

Working with Equations

Many of the fundamental principles in physical science are expressed mathematically in the form of equations. As in any equations, the terms on the left side of a scientific equation are equal to the terms on the right side. However, unlike purely mathematical equations, which may involve equalities between pure numbers, equations used in physical science show how different physical quantities are related to one another.

You can manipulate the terms in a scientific equation using algebra. This is helpful when you need to isolate one quantity in particular, such as when it is the unknown variable in a problem. For example, the following equation is a mathematical expression of the physical principle known as Newton's second law (you will study the implications of this law later):

$$net\ force = mass \times acceleration$$

$$F_{net} = ma$$

Using algebra, you can come up with two different, but equivalent, forms of this equation:

1) $acceleration = \dfrac{net\ force}{mass}$ $a = \dfrac{F_{net}}{m}$

2) $mass = \dfrac{net\ force}{acceleration}$ $m = \dfrac{F_{net}}{a}$

When you are using equations to solve a problem in physical science, it is usually best to rearrange the equations to isolate the unknown variable on the left side *before* you plug in the known values for the other variables.

Vectors

A **vector** is a quantity that has both a magnitude and a direction. One example of a vector quantity is *force*, which is a push or pull on an object. If you are pushing a box along the floor, there are two aspects to the force with which you are pushing: the magnitude—how hard you are pushing—and the direction you are pushing.

If you are only studying motion or forces in one dimension (along a line), you can represent the direction of a vector by making the magnitude positive or negative. However, a more general way to specify the direction of a vector is to use an angle from a fixed reference line. For example, you might push on the box at an angle 30° below horizontal.

Vectors are often depicted visually on diagrams by arrows. The direction the arrow points is the direction of the vector, and the length of the arrow represents the magnitude. The graphical depiction of vector arrows not only helps you visualize a physical situation, it also allows you to approximate the result of adding two or more vectors together. For example, imagine that you and a friend are both pushing on a heavy box. It is hard to push the box straight ahead because you are each at a corner of the box, so you both push at a slight angle. The diagram below shows the two vectors representing the forces with which you push the box. The scale used for the force vectors is 1 cm = 100 N.

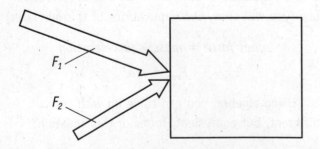

The overall force on the box that results from you and your friend pushing on the box is called the *resultant force*. You can find the length and direction of the resultant vector by placing the two force

vectors end-to-end to make two sides of a triangle. The resultant vector is the third side of the triangle.

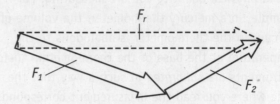

As the diagram above shows, in this case the resultant vector (F_r) is horizontal. If you measure the length of this resultant vector, you will find that it is 6.5 cm long. Because the scale used for the vectors is 1 cm = 100 N, you can therefore conclude that the resultant force on the box has a magnitude of 650 N.

Resolving Vectors into Components

A more exact method of adding vectors involves separating the vectors into horizontal and vertical components. This involves placing (or simply imagining) each vector on an *x-y* axis system. For example, consider the same situation as above, you and a friend pushing a box. Let's start by looking at F_2. Say that we know that F_2 is at an angle 30.0° above horizontal, and has a magnitude of 288 N.

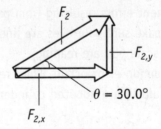

We can now find the magnitudes of the horizontal and vertical components of the vector using sines and cosines. For the horizontal component, $F_{2,x}$, we know the following:

$$\frac{F_{2,x}}{F_2} = \cos 30.0°$$

Therefore, we can find the magnitude of $F_{2,x}$ as follows:

$$F_{2,x} = F_2 \cos 30.0°$$

$$F_{2,x} = (288 \text{ N})(0.866) = 249 \text{ N}$$

Similarly, we can find the magnitude of the vertical component, $F_{2,y}$ as follows:

$$\frac{F_{2,y}}{F_2} = \sin 30.0°$$

$$F_{2,y} = F_2 \sin 30.0°$$

$$F_{2,y} = (288 \text{ N})(0.500) = 144 \text{ N}$$

We could use the same process to find the horizontal and vertical components of F_1. If we know that F_1 has a magnitude of 421 N and is at an angle 20.0° below horizontal ($\theta = -20.0°$), then the calculations are as follows:

$$F_{1,x} = F_1 \cos(-20.0°)$$

$$F_{1,x} = (421 \text{ N})(0.940) = 396 \text{ N}$$

and

$$F_{1,y} = F_1 \sin(-20.0°)$$

$$F_{1,y} = (421 \text{ N})(-0.342) = -144 \text{ N}$$

Now we can find the horizontal component of the resultant vector by adding the horizontal components of F_1 and F_2:

$$F_{r,x} = F_{1,x} + F_{2,x}$$

$$F_{r,x} = (396 \text{ N}) + (249 \text{ N}) = 645 \text{ N}$$

We can also find the vertical component of the resultant vector as follows:

$$F_{r,y} = F_{1,y} + F_{2,y}$$

$$F_{r,y} = (-144 \text{ N}) + (144 \text{ N}) = 0 \text{ N}$$

Because the vertical component is zero, we know the resultant vector is horizontal, and has a total magnitude of 645 N. This is close to the magnitude we found before by placing the vectors end-to-end, but it is more exact.

Note that in cases where neither of the components of the resultant vector are zero, you can find the magnitude of the resultant using the Pythagorean theorem:

$$F_r^2 = F_{r,x}^2 + F_{r,y}^2$$

$$F_r = \sqrt{F_{r,x}^2 + F_{r,y}^2}$$

You can also find the angle of the resultant vector using an inverse tangent:

$$\theta_r = \tan^{-1}\left(\frac{F_{r,y}}{F_{r,x}}\right)$$

UNIT 1   Review

Darken the circle by the correct answer.

1. What is the name of the system of units used by most scientists around the world?

   (A) the British system

   (B) the U.S. system

   (C) the French system

   (D) the Système Internationale

2. Which of the following units are equivalent to 10^{-3} V?

   (A) MV

   (B) kV

   (C) mV

   (D) μV

3. Conversion factors

   (A) are used to switch from one system of units to another.

   (B) are used to switch from one power-of-ten to another.

   (C) are always equal to 1.

   (D) All of the above.

4. When multiplying numbers in scientific notation,

   (A) add the initial numbers and multiply the exponents on the powers of ten.

   (B) multiply the initial numbers and add the exponents on the powers of ten.

   (C) multiply both the initial numbers and the exponents on the powers of ten.

   (D) multiply the initial numbers and do nothing to the power of ten.

5. Which of the following distance measurements has the fewest number of significant figures?

   (A) 20 cm

   (B) 0.00074 m

   (C) 1,360 km

   (D) 3.75×10^5 km

6. Which of the following distance measurements has the least precision?

   (A) 20 cm

   (B) 0.00074 m

   (C) 1,360 km

   (D) 3.75×10^5 km

7. You are trying to measure a volume of water using a glass container. The surface of the water forms a curved meniscus. Where should you take the volume reading?

   (A) at the edges of the meniscus

   (B) at the bottom of the meniscus

   (C) at the top of the meniscus

   (D) halfway between the bottom and the top of the meniscus

8. What kind of quantity has both magnitude and direction?

   (A) a physical quantity

   (B) an analog quantity

   (C) a variable

   (D) a vector

Review (cont'd.)

~~~~~~

9. Rearrange the equation $KE = \frac{1}{2}mv^2$ to solve for v. Show your work.

_____

10. 2.54 cm = 1 in. and 1 m = 100 cm. How many inches are in a meter? Show your work.

_____

UNIT 1    Units of Measurement

> In order to make communication between scientists around the world easier, most scientists use units of measurement from the **Système Internationale** (International System), abbreviated "SI."

Match the quantities below to their SI units.

Quantity

1. Distance/length _____

2. Time _____

3. Speed _____

4. Mass _____

5. Volume _____

6. Area _____

7. Density _____

8. Force _____

9. Electric charge _____

10. Energy _____

Units

A. kg

B. m

C. s

D. N

E. J

F. C

G. m/s

H. m^2

I. m^3

J. kg/m^3

UNIT 1

Converting Units

Conversions Between British/U.S. and SI Units	
British/U.S. System	**SI**
1 in.	2.54 cm
1 ft	0.305 m
1 mi	1.61 km
1 qt	0.946 L
1 lb	4.448 N

Powers-of-Ten Prefixes		
Power	**Prefix**	**Abbreviation**
10^6	mega-	M
10^3	kilo-	k
10^{-2}	centi-	c
10^{-3}	milli-	m
10^{-6}	micro-	μ
10^{-9}	nano-	n

Converting from one set of units to another involves multiplying by a conversion factor—a ratio of units that is equal to 1. Use the tables to find conversion factors to make the conversions specified below.

1. 745 mm = _____ m

2. 100 m = _____ km

3. 3.51×10^{-7} s = _____ ns

4. 4.5 mg = _____ kg

5. 25 μm = _____ m

6. 1200 MJ = _____ J

7. 5 mA = _____ A

8. 12 V = _____ kV

9. 15 in. = _____ cm

10. 15 mi = _____ km

11. 95 km = _____ mi

12. 125 lb = _____ N

13. 20.5 N = _____ lb

14. exactly 1 gal (4 qt) = _____ L

15. exactly 100 yd (300 ft) = _____ m

16. 750 mL = _____ qt

17. 75 km/h = _____ mi/h

18. 75 km/h = _____ m/s

19. 35 mi/h = _____ km/h

20. 35 mi/h = _____ m/s

UNIT 1

Scientific Notation

> *Numbers in scientific notation have one nonzero digit to the left of the decimal point, the remaining digits to the right of the decimal point, and are multiplied by a power of ten. For example, the number 325,000 would be written as 3.25×10^5 in scientific notation.*

Convert the following numbers to scientific notation.

1. 1,200 _____

2. 0.0012 _____

3. 57 _____

4. 3.5 million _____

5. 6 _____

6. Write 1.47×10^3 m/s, the speed of sound in water, in standard notation.

   _____

7. Write the diameter of an atom, 1×10^{-8} cm, in standard notation.

   _____

8. The distance from Earth to the moon is about 3.84×10^5 km. Express this number in standard notation.

   _____

9. Write the mass of an electron, 0.000 549 amu, in scientific notation.

   _____

10. The area of the Pacific Ocean is 166 000 000 km², and the ocean's average depth is 4200 m. Write these numbers in scientific notation.

    _____

11. In meteorology, 0.005 cm/h of precipitation is a mist, while 0.02 cm/h of precipitation is a drizzle. Write these numbers in scientific notation.

    _____

    _____

12. Humans can hear sounds with frequencies up to 20 000 Hz, while dolphins can hear sounds as high as 150 000 Hz. Write these numbers in scientific notation.

    _____

    _____

UNIT 1

Significant Figures

Write the number of significant figures in each of the following quantities. If the number of significant figures is ambiguous, write the minimum number of significant figures.

1. 2 m/s _____

2. 3.5 kg _____

3. 0.73 km _____

4. 0.005 g _____

5. 6.05×10^5 L _____

6. 5900 ft _____

7. 1600.00 m _____

8. 2.0×10^1 N _____

Perform the following calculations. Write the answers with the correct units and the correct number of significant figures.

9. 8.25 cm $\times$ 3.45 cm

10. 58.55 kg $\times$ 9.81 m/s^2

11. 4.135 m $\times$ 4.688 m $\times$ 8.7 m

12. $\dfrac{128 \text{ km}}{2 \text{ h}}$

13. 6.25 kg $-$ 3.55 kg

14. 4.135 m + 4.688 m + 8.7 m

15. 14.75 m + 25 cm

16. 1.0 L + 275 mL

UNIT 1    Taking Measurements

Write the measurement being taken in each of the pictures below. Be sure to include the units of measurement and the correct number of significant figures.

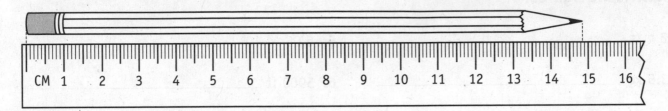

1. _____

2. _____

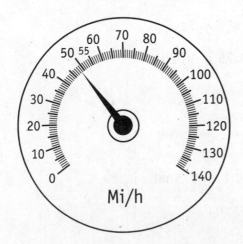

3. _____

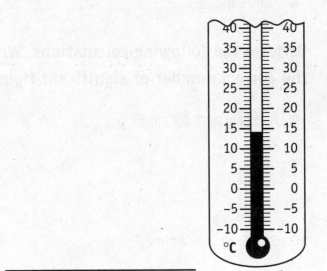

4. _____

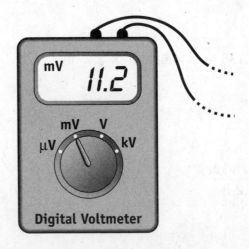

Digital Voltmeter

5. _____

Unit 1, Tools of Physical Science
Physical Science, SV 0425-5

Taking Measurements (cont'd.)

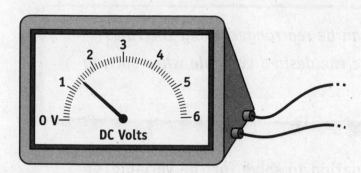

6. _____

7. Which of the instruments shown are digital instruments?

_____

_____

8. Which of the instruments shown are analog instruments?

_____

_____

UNIT 1

Working with Equations

> *Equations used in physical science can be rearranged using the rules of algebra. This allows you to isolate the desired variable when solving a problem.*

For each equation below, rearrange the equation to solve for the variable(s) shown at right.

1. $F_g = mg$ $m =$ _____

2. $F = -kx$ $x =$ _____

3. $V = IR$ $R =$ _____ $I =$ _____

4. $v = \dfrac{d}{t}$ $d =$ _____ $t =$ _____

5. $a = \dfrac{v_f - v_i}{t}$ $v_f =$ _____ $v_i =$ _____

6. $T_F = \dfrac{9}{5}T_C + 32$ $T_C =$ _____

7. $a_c = \dfrac{v^2}{r}$ $r =$ _____ $v =$ _____

8. $KE = \dfrac{1}{2}mv^2$ $m =$ _____ $v =$ _____

9. $F_g = G\dfrac{m_1 m_2}{r^2}$ $m_2 =$ _____ $r =$ _____

10. $mgh = \dfrac{1}{2}mv^2$ $h =$ _____ $v =$ _____

UNIT 1

Vectors

Vectors are quantities with both magnitude and direction. Vectors can be represented graphically using arrows. The length of the arrow corresponds to the magnitude of the vector, and the direction of the arrow is the direction of the vector. Vectors displayed in this way can be added by placing them end-to-end. Vectors can also be added by resolving the vectors into horizontal and vertical components.

On the diagrams below, draw the vector that results from adding the vectors shown.

1. 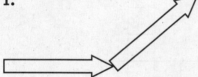   2. 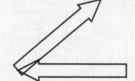   3.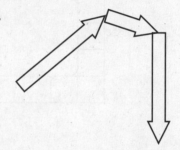

The diagram below shows the velocity vector of a long-jumper just as she starts her jump. The magnitude of the vector is 9.0 m/s, and its direction is 30° above horizontal and in the positive direction.

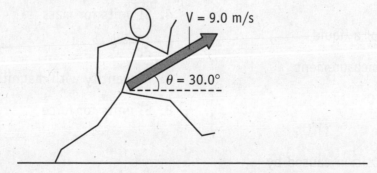

V = 9.0 m/s

$\theta = 30.0°$

4. What is the magnitude of the horizontal component of the velocity, v_x? _____

5. What is the magnitude of the vertical component of the velocity, v_y? _____

UNIT 1

Tools of Physical Science Crossword

ACROSS

1. How close a measurement is to the actual value

3. The curved surface of a liquid

5. The exactness of a measurement

9. Has the form $A \times 10^x$

10. SI units for distance

11. Apparent shift in position caused by changing viewing angle

DOWN

2. A ratio between units that equals 1

4. SI units for mass

6. 10^{-9} s

7. A quantity with magnitude and direction

8. SI units for force

Unit 1, Tools of Physical Science
Physical Science, SV 0425-5

UNIT 2

Although you may not realize it, you have been making observations and thinking scientifically about the physical world for most of your life. For example, you learned at an early age that when you toss something up in the air, it almost always falls back down. Now, without even doing it, you can predict that when you toss something up it will come back down.

With physics, you can describe the motion of objects more exactly by using mathematical equations. These equations are often expressions of physical laws—principles that have been verified through a large number of experiments and, in many cases, common experiences.

Speed

Speed is a measurement of how fast an object moves. Speed is defined as the distance an object moves in a given time interval. This can be expressed with the following equation:

$$speed = \frac{distance}{time}$$

$$v = \frac{d}{t}$$

For example, a car traveling on a highway at 65 miles per hour (mph) will go 65 miles in the time interval of one hour.

Technically, this definition is for *average speed*. The car on the highway may actually go a little bit faster or slower within that time interval, but its overall, average speed is 65 mph. The exact speed of the car in a specific instant is called *instantaneous speed*. Instantaneous speed tells you how far the car *would* go if it continued traveling at that speed for an extended time.

The standard SI units for speed are meters per second (m/s). Other common units for speed are kilometers per hour (km/h) and miles per hour (mph).

Key Terms

speed (v)—a measurement of the distance an object moves in a given time interval

velocity (v)—a vector quantity that measures both speed and direction of motion

acceleration (a)—a vector quantity that measures the change in velocity over a given time interval

projectile motion—the motion of an object influenced only by gravity

centripetal acceleration (a_c)—acceleration directed toward the center of a circular path

Velocity

Sometimes, it is important to distinguish between speed and **velocity**. You can think of velocity as a combination of speed and direction. For example, to describe the velocity of a car on a highway, you might say the car is traveling at 65 mph *to the east*. In other words, velocity is a vector, and the magnitude of velocity is equivalent to speed. Incidentally, this is why "*v*" is often used to represent "speed" in equations.

For one-dimensional motion (motion along a straight line), the direction of motion can be specified by the sign (positive or negative) of the velocity. For example, on a highway, you could define the positive direction as toward the east. A car traveling east would then have positive velocity, while a car going west would have negative velocity.

Acceleration

Objects moving at a constant speed in one direction are moving with *constant velocity*. However, most objects in motion eventually change either their speed, their direction, or both. The quantity that measures the change in velocity over a time interval is **acceleration**.

For motion along a straight line, acceleration can be expressed with the following equation:

$$acceleration = \frac{final\ velocity - initial\ velocity}{time}$$

$$a = \frac{v_f - v_i}{t}$$

The standard SI units for acceleration are m/s². It may help you to think of this as "meters per second per second." For example, a car that accelerates from a speed of 12 m/s to a speed of 14 m/s during one second is changing speed at a rate of 2 m/s per second. In other words, it has an acceleration of 2 m/s².

Like velocity, acceleration is a vector, so it includes both magnitude and direction. For motion in one dimension, the direction of acceleration can be

signified by using a positive or negative sign, just like velocity. If an object moving with positive velocity has a negative acceleration, that means the object is slowing down, or decelerating.

There are several other equations that you can use to analyze constant acceleration along a straight line. Here are some of the most useful ones:

$$d = \frac{1}{2}(v_i - v_f)t$$

$$d = v_i t + \frac{1}{2}at^2$$

$$v_f^2 = v_i^2 + 2ad$$

In these equations, v_i is the initial speed, v_f is the final speed, a is acceleration, t is the time interval, and d is the distance traveled.

Free-Fall Acceleration

An object falling straight down due to gravity near Earth's surface is said to be in *free fall*. Free-fall acceleration, g, is more or less constant near Earth's surface:

$$g = -9.81\ m/s^2$$

That means that the downward velocity of an object in free fall will increase (or the upward velocity will decrease) by 9.81 m/s for every second that it falls. g has a negative value because in most cases it makes sense to define "up" as the positive direction when doing a problem involving free-fall acceleration.

Because free-fall acceleration is constant acceleration in one dimension (the vertical dimension),

you can use all the normal equations for constant acceleration when studying free fall. In each of those equations, just substitute g for a to make the equation apply to free-fall acceleration.

In theory, the rate of free-fall acceleration is the same for any object near Earth's surface, regardless of the mass, volume, or shape of the object. However, in reality, the acceleration for different falling objects might be different due to air resistance. When solving problems involving free-fall acceleration, you can usually assume that air resistance is negligible.

Projectile Motion

The typical equations for speed and acceleration are specifically for one-dimensional motion, or motion along a straight line. However, you can also use these same equations to study two-dimensional motion, or motion in a plane.

For example, you may want to study or describe the motion of a soccer ball, as shown below. Once the soccer ball has been kicked, the ball moves in **projectile motion.** A *projectile* is an object on which the only influence is gravity. The path of a projectile's motion has the shape of a parabola.

To study projectile motion, you have to think about horizontal motion and vertical motion separately. In the horizontal direction, the soccer ball travels with a constant horizontal speed (ignoring air resistance). In the vertical direction—parallel to the y–axis—the ball is subject to Earth's gravity, and so has a constant downward acceleration of g, or -9.81 m/s^2.

The initial velocity of the soccer ball, v_i, is shown on the diagram as a vector—an arrow at an angle, θ, above the x–axis. The next step is to separate this initial velocity vector into horizontal and vertical components:

Horizontal component: $v_{x,i} = v_i\cos\theta$

Vertical component: $v_{y,i} = v_i\sin\theta$

Once you have separated the velocity into horizontal and vertical components, you can use the equations for speed and acceleration in one dimension. For example, if you want to find the speed and direction of the soccer ball after a time interval, t, you start by finding the vertical and horizontal velocities separately. For the vertical component, use the equation for acceleration (rearranged to solve for final velocity) to find the final vertical velocity:

$$v_{y,f} = v_{y,i} + at$$

The acceleration in this case is free-fall acceleration, so $a = g = -9.81$ m/s^2.

The horizontal component is easy: the final horizontal velocity is the same as the initial horizontal velocity, because the horizontal speed is constant.

$$v_{x,f} = v_{x,i}$$

To translate from these component velocities back into the final velocity of the ball, v_f, you use the Pythagorean theorem:

$$v_f = \sqrt{v_{x,f}^2 + v_{y,f}^2}$$

To find the ball's final direction—an angle, θ_f, from the x–axis—you use an inverse tangent:

$$\theta_f = \tan^{-1}\left(\frac{v_{y,f}}{v_{x,f}}\right)$$

Note that this inverse tangent method will work whether the direction is angled upward or downward.

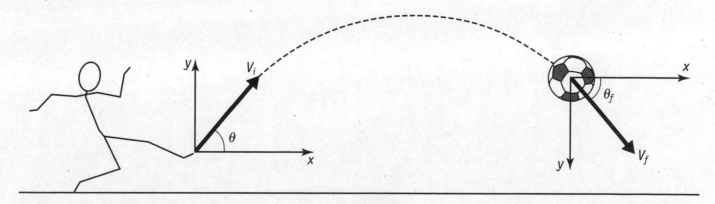

If θ_f is negative, that means the angle is below the x–axis, so the ball is moving at a downward angle.

Using component vectors like this, you can calculate quite a lot about the ball's motion, including the time the ball is in the air, how high the ball rises, how far it travels horizontally, and its velocity at any point.

Circular Motion

An object can accelerate without changing its speed. For example, a ball whirled on the end of a string may move at a constant speed, but it is always accelerating—changing velocity—because the *direction* of motion is continually changing.

Acceleration that causes an object to move in a circle is called centripetal acceleration. The direction of **centripetal acceleration** is perpendicular to the motion of the object and points toward the center of the circle. The velocity of the object as it travels in a circle is called the *tangential velocity*, and its direction is in a straight line tangent to the circular path. Because centripetal acceleration is perpendicular to tangential velocity, it doesn't cause any change in the magnitude of the tangential velocity. In other words, centripetal acceleration involves a change in direction, but not a change in speed.

You can calculate the magnitude of centripetal acceleration from the tangential speed of the object and the radius of the circle:

$$centripetal\ acceleration = \frac{(speed)^2}{radius}$$

$$a_c = \frac{v^2}{r}$$

You can also use this equation for the curved motion of an object, even if the object doesn't complete an entire circle. For example, imagine a car traveling around a curve that approximates an arc on a circle, as shown below. The curve doesn't go in a complete circle, but you can imagine the curve as part of a circle. To find the centripetal acceleration of the car, you have to know a property of the curve called the *radius of curvature*—the radius of the circle that the curve *would* complete if it continued in a full circle.

Once you know the radius of curvature, you can use it as the radius in the equation for centripetal acceleration. So, for example, if the car is traveling at 15 m/s, and the radius of curvature for the curve is 75 m, you can calculate the centripetal acceleration:

$$a_c = \frac{v^2}{r} = \frac{(15\ m/s)^2}{75\ m} = 3.0\ m/s^2$$

Note that the units in the equation work out to give the final answer in units of m/s².

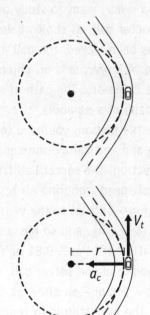

UNIT 2

Review

Darken the circle by the correct answer.

1. What measures the distance an object travels in a given time interval?

Ⓐ average speed

Ⓑ instantaneous speed

Ⓒ acceleration

Ⓓ projectile motion

2. The exact speed of an object in a specific instant is

Ⓐ average speed.

Ⓑ instantaneous speed.

Ⓒ acceleration.

Ⓓ projectile motion.

3. What quantity expresses both speed and direction?

Ⓐ average speed

Ⓑ velocity

Ⓒ acceleration

Ⓓ centripetal acceleration

4. What are the standard units for acceleration?

Ⓐ m/s

Ⓑ m•s

Ⓒ m/s^2

Ⓓ m/s^3

5. Free-fall acceleration

Ⓐ depends on the mass of the falling object.

Ⓑ depends on the height from which an object falls.

Ⓒ is constant near Earth's surface.

Ⓓ has horizontal and vertical components.

6. An object in projectile motion

Ⓐ follows the path of a hyperbola.

Ⓑ accelerates without changing its speed.

Ⓒ accelerates in the vertical and horizontal dimensions.

Ⓓ has a constant acceleration directed downward.

7. What is the direction of centripetal acceleration?

Ⓐ the same as the direction of velocity

Ⓑ directly opposite the direction of velocity

Ⓒ perpendicular to velocity and towards the center

Ⓓ Centripetal acceleration has no direction.

8. Explain how an object can accelerate without changing its speed. Give one example of a situation in which this occurs.

_____

_____

_____

_____

UNIT 2    Speed and Velocity

> Speed is a quantity that measures the distance an object travels in a given time interval.
>
> $$speed = \frac{distance}{time} \qquad v = \frac{d}{t}$$
>
> Velocity is a vector that includes speed and direction.

Answer the following questions about speed and velocity.

1. A car is driving west on a highway at 25 m/s. What is the car's speed in km/h?

_____

2. What is the car's velocity?

_____

_____

3. If the positive direction is defined as "toward the east," what is a mathematical expression of the car's velocity?

_____

4. How far does the car travel in 5 minutes? Express your answer in m and km.

_____

5. Polar bears are extremely good swimmers and can travel as long as 10 hours without resting. If a polar bear swims with an average speed of 2.6 m/s, how far does it travel in 10.0 hours? Express your answer in m and km.

_____

6. Suppose the polar bear were running on land instead of swimming. If the polar bear runs at an average speed of 8.3 m/s, how far does it travel in 10.0 hours? Express your answer in m and km.

_____

7. A walrus can swim faster than a polar bear, but has less endurance. If a walrus swims at an average speed of 9.7 m/s, how far does the walrus swim in 3.4 minutes? Express your answer in m and km.

_____

8. Tree sloths are the slowest mammals on Earth. An typical tree sloth moves with a maximum speed of 0.075 m/s. How long would it take a sloth moving at this speed to travel 2.0 m?

_____

_____

UNIT 2  Graphing Speed

Use the following information to answer questions about graphing speed.

Jesse Owens won four gold medals in the 1936 Olympic Games in Berlin. One of these was for the 100 m dash, in which Owens tied the Olympic record with a time of 10.3 s.

1. Using the data from the first two columns in the table below, plot a graph of distance versus time for a sprinter in the 100 m dash.

Time (s)	Total distance (m)	Average speed (m/s)
1.0	4.0	
2.0	10	
3.0	18	
4.0	27	
5.0	37	
6.0	48	
7.0	59	
8.0	71	
9.0	83	
10.0	96	
10.3	100	

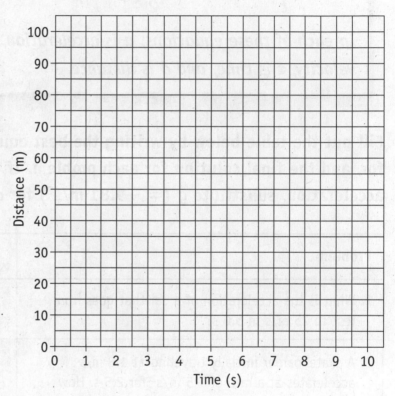

2. How does the slope of the line on the graph change with increasing time?

_____

_____

3. What is the slope of the line in the interval in which the slope is greatest? _____

4. What are the units of this slope? _____

5. Complete the table by calculating the average speed in each time interval.

6. What is the relationship between average speed and the slope on the graph?

UNIT 2

Acceleration

Here are several equations that can be used to describe and study the motion of objects moving with a constant acceleration in a straight line, including free-fall acceleration:

$$a = \frac{(v_f - v_i)}{t} \qquad d = \frac{1}{2}(v_i - v_f)t \qquad d = v_i t + \frac{1}{2}at^2 \qquad v_f^2 = v_i^2 + 2ad$$

In each of these equations, a is acceleration, v_i is initial velocity, v_f is final velocity, t is time, and d is distance.

Fill out the table below by writing the best equation to use, the variable to solve for, and the final solution for each problem. If the problem involves free-fall acceleration, substitute g (= -9.81 m/s^2) for a in the equation.

Problem	Equation used	Variable solving for	Solution
1. What is the acceleration of a car that goes from rest to 25 m/s in 5.0 s?			
2. A skateboarder initially traveling at 1.8 m/s accelerates at a rate of 1.5 m/s² for 2.5 s. How far does the skateboarder go in this time?			
3. A cyclist slows from 15 m/s to 3.0 m/s over a distance of 36 m. How long does this take?			
4. A monkey throws a coconut from a height of 4.0 m and with an initial speed of 3.5 m/s. What is the speed of the coconut when it hits the ground?			
5. A tennis player tosses a ball straight up for a serve. The ball's initial speed is 5.0 m/s. How high does the ball rise above the tennis player's hand?	$v_f^2 = v_i^2 + 2gd$		

UNIT 2 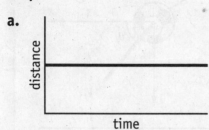 Speed and Acceleration Graphs

Match the following graphs to the kind of motion they describe.

Graph	Kind of motion

Graph

a.

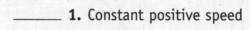

b.

c.

d.

e.

Kind of motion

_____ **1.** Constant positive speed

_____ **2.** Constant negative speed

_____ **3.** Constant positive acceleration

_____ **4.** Constant negative acceleration

_____ **5.** Object at rest

UNIT 2

Projectile Motion

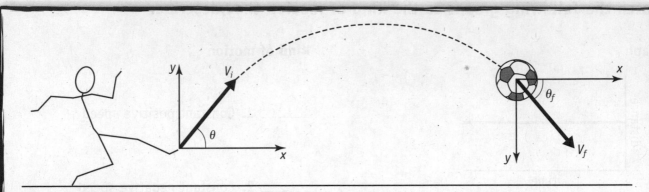

A soccer ball has been kicked with an initial velocity of 15 m/s at an angle 60° above the horizontal. Assume that air resistance is negligible, so the only influence on the ball after it has been kicked is the acceleration due to gravity ($g = -9.81$ m/s²).

Answer the following questions about the projectile motion of the ball.

1. Will the horizontal velocity of the ball change during the projectile motion? _____

2. Will the vertical velocity of the ball change during the projectile motion? _____

3. What is the initial horizontal velocity of the ball? _____

4. What is the initial vertical velocity of the ball? _____

5. What is the horizontal velocity of the ball after 2.0 s? _____

6. What is the vertical velocity of the ball after 2.0 s? _____

7. What is the total speed of the ball after 2.0 s? (Hint: Use the Pythagorean Theorem.) _____

8. What is the angle of the ball's velocity after 2.0 s? (Hint: Use an inverse tangent.) _____

9. Has the ball yet reached its maximum height after 2.0 s? How can you tell this from the angle? _____

10. How long does it take for the ball to reach its maximum height? (Hint: Rearrange the standard equation for acceleration to solve for t. At the maximum height, $v_{y,f} = 0$ m/s.)

_____

11. How high is the ball when it reaches its maximum height? (Hint: One way to do this is to rearrange the following to solve for d: $v_f^2 = v_i^2 + 2ad$.) _____

UNIT 2  Centripetal Acceleration

Centripetal acceleration is acceleration directed toward the center of a circular path.

$$\text{centripetal acceleration} = \frac{(speed)^2}{radius} \qquad a_c = \frac{v^2}{r}$$

You can also calculate centripetal acceleration for an object moving on any curved path by using the radius of curvature.

Answer the following questions about centripetal acceleration.

1. On the diagram below, draw and label the following: centripetal acceleration, tangential velocity, radius of curvature.

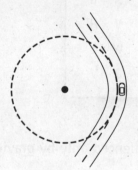

2. Describe the relationship between the direction of centripetal acceleration and the direction of tangential velocity.

_____

_____

_____

3. How would the magnitude of the centripetal acceleration change if the tangential speed of the car doubled?

_____

_____

_____

4. Calculate the centripetal acceleration if the car is traveling at 18 m/s and the radius of curvature is 45 m.

_____

5. If the centripetal acceleration is 3.5 m/s² when the tangential speed of the car is 15 m/s, what is the radius of curvature?

_____

6. If the radius of curvature is 25 m, how fast would the car have to go to have a centripetal acceleration of 5.0 m/s²?

_____

UNIT 2

Motion Word Find

Find the answers to the following in the word find puzzle below.

```
F K F M S O H N O Q A W N K U
A R O O N V U O L J T J V O Y
G T E H A N Q I E E D W L Q H
C S T E U J Z T P O E E V W Z
E Q B Z F R E A F Z E G B J P
N F X W O A P R H M P R R A H
T P Y X R C L E I M S H R S B
R B T L B U C L O Y U A C K E
I B I O G K O E Z C B Y B T W
P W C A B B Z C Y O R O G L B
E Q O Y R N Y C L Y X D C X V
T U L W G A C A Z D W P H X B
A W E Z O H D X V B J A C V H
L T V Y E H C P B U Y E E W I
E L I T C E J O R P X Q Z J V
```

1. Measures distance traveled in a given time interval

_____

2. Includes speed and direction

_____

3. Measures the rate of change of velocity

_____

4. Describes the motion of objects affected by gravity near Earth's surface

_____

5. An object influenced only by gravity

_____

6. The shape of a projectile's path

_____

7. Describes acceleration directed toward the center of a circular path

_____

UNIT 3  Force

You can describe the motion of objects using equations or graphs representing speed and acceleration. However, these analytical tools do not explain *why* objects move the way they do. The underlying principles that explain motion and changes in motion were first presented formally by Isaac Newton. These principles are now known as Newton's laws.

Newton's First Law

Newton's first law states:

> *An object at rest will remain at rest and an object in motion will remain in motion at a constant velocity unless an unbalanced force acts on the object.*

The tendency for an object to maintain its state of motion is called **inertia**. Newton's first law is also sometimes called the *law of inertia*. This law also introduces another new term: **force**. In simple terms, a force is a push or a pull on an object. Newton's second law, which we will get to shortly, deals with force more directly.

The inertia of objects at rest is very easy to understand, and we observe it all the time. If you set a book down on a flat table, you know the book won't start moving on its own. The book will remain at rest until some external, unbalanced force acts on it, like your hand picking it up again.

The inertia of moving objects can be harder to grasp because it is contrary to much of our everyday experience. Most objects that we observe in motion will eventually come to rest unless some additional force is applied to keep them moving. However, this happens because there usually is some other unbalanced force acting on the object, such as the

Key Terms

inertia—the tendency for an object to remain at rest or to continue moving at a constant velocity unless acted upon by an unbalanced force

force (F)—the cause of an object's acceleration; a vector quantity equal to the product of the object's mass and its acceleration

mass (m)—a measure of the amount of matter in an object

momentum (p)—a vector quantity equal to the product of an object's mass and its velocity

impulse—a vector quantity equal to force multiplied by a time interval

normal force (F_n)—a reaction force perpendicular to the surface of contact between two objects

weight (F_g)—the force of gravity on an object

centripetal force (F_c)—any force that causes centripetal acceleration, or acceleration that results in a curved path of motion

density (D)—a measurement of mass per unit volume

buoyant force (F_B)—the upward force that a fluid exerts on a submerged or floating object

friction (F_f)—a force that opposes motion between two surfaces that are in contact

static friction (F_s)—the friction between two contacting surfaces that are at rest relative to one another

kinetic friction (F_k)—the friction between two contacting surfaces that are moving relative to one another

force of friction. For example, if you push a book along a tabletop, the book will move only a short distance before friction between the book and the table brings the book to a stop.

The inertia of moving objects is more apparent when you think about how objects move in outer space, where there are fewer forces acting on objects. For example, if an astronaut pushes a book so it moves away from him at a small speed, it will keep moving with that speed, and in the same direction, until it hits a wall, or perhaps until another astronaut catches it. Spacecraft like Voyagers 1 and 2, which are now currently headed out of our solar system, can continue moving at a constant speed in a straight line more or less indefinitely without any additional propulsion.

When a car enters a turn going at a fairly high speed, the passengers may feel as if they are being pulled toward the outside edge of the turn. This is also inertia; the bodies of the passengers have a tendency to keep moving in a straight line. The passengers only stay in their seats because the force of friction between their bodies and the seats (and perhaps also the force of an arm pushing against a door) causes them to move in a curved motion along with the car.

Mass and Momentum

Mass is a measure of the amount of matter in an object. Sometimes, mass is also defined as a measure of an object's inertia, or its tendency to resist acceleration. The SI unit for mass is kilograms (kg).

Momentum is a concept closely related to mass and inertia. In simple terms, momentum tells you how hard it is to stop the motion of an object. We use the term *momentum* to describe things outside of scientific contexts, too. For example, if a sports team has a lot of momentum, then they are "on a roll," and it is harder to stop them from scoring.

Quantitatively, momentum is defined as the product of an object's mass and its velocity:

$$momentum = mass \times velocity$$

$$p = mv$$

The SI units of momentum are kg•m/s. Momentum is a vector that has the same direction as the object's velocity. Note that an object can have a large momentum by having a large mass, a high velocity, or both.

Momentum is a *conserved quantity*, which means that no matter what happens, the total amount of momentum remains the same. This is formalized in the law of conservation of momentum:

The total momentum of an isolated system always remains constant.

The law of conservation of momentum is particularly useful for studying collisions. If you know the momentum of each object in a collision before the collision happens, you can predict the momentum of each object (and therefore their velocities) after the collision. The total momentum of the system will remain the same.

Newton's Second Law

While Newton's first law explains what happens when no forces act on an object, Newton's second law is concerned with what happens when forces do act on an object. In words, Newton's second law states:

The net force on an object is directly proportional to the object's mass and acceleration, and has the same direction as the object's acceleration.

Quantitatively, Newton's second law is stated with the following equation:

$$net\ force = mass \times acceleration$$

$$F_{net} = ma$$

From the equation, you might guess that the units of force would be kg•m/s^2. These are valid units for force, but more often, scientists use equivalent SI units called, appropriately, newtons (N). A newton is the amount of force required to accelerate a 1 kg object at a rate of 1 m/s^2. Like velocity and acceleration, force is a vector, so it has both a magnitude and a direction.

Newton's second law tells us more than just a mathematical relationship between force and acceleration. It also tells us that acceleration is always accompanied by a net force. More strongly, one can say that force *causes* acceleration. Newton's second law also encompasses his first law, because the first law essentially says that acceleration is zero when the net force is zero.

There are many different kinds of forces. Some examples are gravitational force, the force of electrical attraction or repulsion, friction, and simply the force of one object pushing on another. Newton's second law applies no matter what kind of forces are involved in a situation.

Note, however, that the force in Newton's second law is specified as the *net* force. That means you can apply the law only after you have found the resulting sum of all the forces acting on an object. If there are several forces acting in the same direction, they will sum together to make a larger net force. If some of the forces on an object are acting in opposite directions, they will cancel each other out to some degree, or perhaps even completely cancel each other.

The Impulse-Momentum Theorem

Because forces cause acceleration, forces also cause changes in momentum. The relationship between force and momentum is expressed by the impulse-momentum theorem:

$$impulse = change\ in\ momentum$$

$$Ft = \Delta p$$

As this equation shows, **impulse** is a quantity defined as force multiplied by time. Note also that the "delta" (Δ) on the right side of the equation is a Greek letter meaning "change."

The impulse-momentum theorem shows that the magnitude of a force is not the only factor in changing an object's momentum. The length of time over which the force acts on an object is also important. A small force applied for a long time can cause a large change in momentum.

This principle is used in some recent spacecraft propulsion systems. For example, Deep Space 1, launched in 1998 to intercept the comet Borrelly, used an ion propulsion system that exerted a small force over a long period of time. A similar system might be used in the first manned missions to Mars.

Newton's Third Law

Newton's third law can be stated a number of different ways. Perhaps the most common is the following:

For every action, there is an equal and opposite reaction.

Another way of saying this is:

Forces always occur in action-reaction pairs.

For example, imagine two people—say, Annie and Joe—standing on skateboards and initially at rest. Annie exerts a force on Joe by pushing on his shoulders. This causes Joe to accelerate and start moving away from Annie. However, as Annie's hands exert a force on Joe, there is an equal and opposite force—*a reaction force*—exerted on Annie's hands by Joe's shoulders. This reaction force causes Annie to accelerate and start moving away from Joe as well. You might wonder, do these two forces cancel each other because they are equal and opposite? No, they don't cancel, because the action force and the reaction force are each acting on a different object. The action force acts on Joe, while the reaction force acts on Annie.

Newton's third law is the principle behind the propulsion of rockets. A rocket gets propulsion by burning fuel. When the fuel burns, it expands and is

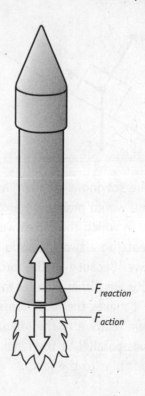

$F_{reaction}$

F_{action}

Physical Science, SV 0425-5

forced out of the bottom of the rocket. The rocket is propelled not by the force pushing on the fuel, but rather by the reaction force, equal and opposite to the force pushing the fuel out. Although these two forces are equal in magnitude, the fuel accelerates to a high speed more quickly because the fuel has less mass than the rocket itself does.

Force Diagrams

Force diagrams are a useful tool for studying the forces acting on an object. A force diagram is simply a diagram that shows the forces acting on an object.

For example, consider the forces acting on a box on a ramp, as shown below. First of all, notice that all the forces are drawn as if they are acting on a point at the center of the box. F_g is the force of gravity, and F_f is the force of friction. We will discuss the force of gravity and the force of friction in more detail later on, but you probably have at least a basic idea of what those are. The **normal force**, F_n, is simply the force of the ramp pushing on the box. This is a reaction force that is equal and opposite to the force of the box pushing on the ramp. In this case, *normal* is just another word for *perpendicular*; normal forces are always perpendicular to the contacting surface between two objects.

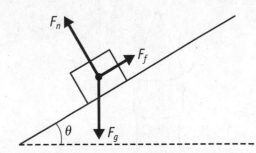

If you were solving a problem involving this box on a ramp, you would probably want to draw another force diagram in which the forces were all resolved into components on a two-dimensional axis system, as shown above. Because all the forces except the force of gravity are either parallel to or perpendicular to the ramp, it makes the most sense to orient the x–y axis system relative to the ramp. In other words, make the x-axis parallel to the ramp, and make the y-axis perpendicular to the ramp.

With the axes aligned in this way, the only force you need to resolve into components is the force of gravity. Here are the equations you would use:

$$F_{g,x} = F_g \sin\theta$$

$$F_{g,y} = F_g \cos\theta$$

In each of these equations, θ is the angle between the force of gravity and the y-axis, which is also equal to the angle of the ramp above the horizontal.

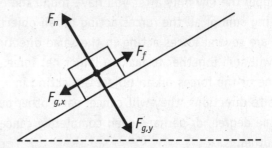

Resolving the force of gravity into components also tells you the magnitude of the normal force; it has the same magnitude (and opposite direction) as the y-component of the force of gravity:

$$F_n = -F_{g,y}$$

Furthermore, if the box is at rest, then you know the force of friction must have the same magnitude (and opposite direction) as the x-component of the force of gravity, so that the net force along the x-axis is zero:

$$F_f = -F_{g,x} \quad \text{(box at rest)}$$

Weight

Another term for the force of gravity on an object (F_g) is **weight**. It is important to understand that mass and weight are not the same thing. Mass is a fundamental property of an object and does not change when the object moves from one location to another. Weight, on the other hand, depends on an object's location. More specifically, weight depends on the value of the free-fall acceleration, *g*, at the object's location.

For example, an astronaut has the same mass when on the moon as when on Earth. However, the astronaut's weight is less on the moon than on Earth.

Earth is more massive than the moon, and therefore exerts a stronger gravitational force.

The weight of an object can be calculated from the object's mass using the following equation:

$$weight = mass \times free\text{-}fall\ acceleration$$

$$F_g = mg$$

In this equation, g is the free-fall acceleration of the object at that point. You may recall that g near Earth's surface is 9.81 m/s². Note that this is just Newton's second law with g substituted for a. Because weight is a force, its SI unit is newtons (N).

Apparent Weightlessness

You may have heard that astronauts experience *weightlessness* when in a space shuttle orbiting Earth. A more appropriate term would be *apparent weightlessness*. You may have briefly experienced a lesser degree of apparent weightlessness when riding in an elevator or on a roller coaster.

An astronaut in orbit still has weight because Earth is still exerting a gravitational force on the astronaut. This force causes the astronaut to accelerate downward (the acceleration is both free-fall acceleration and a centripetal acceleration directed toward Earth). However, the space shuttle is also accelerating downward at the same rate. Because the astronaut and the shuttle are both accelerating at the same rate, the astronaut seems to float weightlessly

in the shuttle. What the astronaut is actually lacking is not weight, but rather the normal force of the ground pushing back.

Universal Gravitation

During Isaac Newton's time, many scientists and philosophers were trying to figure out how the moon, the planets, and Earth itself moved. This was shortly after Copernicus had proposed that Earth and the other planets orbit the sun, rather than the sun and planets orbiting Earth, as was believed previously. Johannes Kepler took Copernicus' ideas further and showed that the orbits of the planets (including Earth) are ellipses, not perfect circles. Kepler also described other, more specific properties of these orbits. However, nobody knew *why* the planets move in elliptical orbits, or why the orbits have the properties they do.

Newton answered many of these questions with his theory of universal gravitation. Newton proposed that *all* objects exert gravitational forces on each other. This was a radical idea at the time, as nobody knew whether the laws of physics as observed on Earth also applied to objects beyond Earth.

Newton's law of universal gravitation is expressed mathematically as follows:

$$force\ of\ gravity = G \times \frac{mass\ 1 \times mass\ 2}{radius^2}$$

$$F_g = G\frac{m_1 m_2}{r^2}$$

In this equation, m_1 and m_2 are the masses of the two objects, r is the distance between the objects (measured from their centers), and G is a constant called the *constant of universal gravitation*. Newton wasn't sure of the exact value of G, but we now know:

$$G = 6.67 \times 10^{-11}\ N \bullet m^2/kg^2$$

You could use Newton's law of universal gravitation to calculate the gravitational force that you exert on the person sitting next to you. (Try it!) If you do so, you will find that the magnitude of the force turns out to be very small, mostly because G is such a small number. The fact that G is small reveals a practical truth: the force of gravity is usually only significant when at least one of the objects is extremely massive (like Earth, for example).

Centripetal Force

In the unit on motion, we discussed a type of acceleration called *centripetal acceleration*. You may recall that centripetal acceleration is the perpendicular acceleration of an object moving in a curved path. You may also recall the equation for the magnitude of centripetal acceleration:

$$centripetal\ acceleration = \frac{(speed)^2}{radius}$$

$$a_c = \frac{v^2}{r}$$

In this equation, *v* is the tangential velocity of the object, and *r* is the radius of an imaginary circle that approximates the curved path. *r* is also called the *radius of curvature*.

A **centripetal force** is simply a force that causes centripetal acceleration. Using a_c for *a* in Newton's second law gives us the equation for the magnitude of centripetal force:

$$F_c = ma_c = m\frac{v^2}{r}$$

$$centripetal\ force = mass \times \frac{(speed)^2}{radius}$$

Like centripetal acceleration, centripetal force is directed perpendicular to the motion of the object, toward the center of an imaginary circle that approximates the curved path of the object.

Centripetal forces can be of many different types. For example, when a car rounds a curve, the centripetal force is friction between the car's tires and the road. This force causes the car to deviate from a straight-line path and to move instead along a curved path. The force of gravity can also be a centripetal force. For example, the gravitational force of Earth on the moon is a centripetal force that causes the moon to move in a nearly circular orbit around Earth. In the case of a ball whirled on a string, the centripetal force is tension in the string.

Density and Buoyancy

The **density** of an object (or any substance) is a measurement of the mass *per unit volume*. In other words, density tells you how much matter is packed into a given amount of space.

The equation for calculating density is:

$$density = \frac{mass}{volume}$$

$$D = \frac{m}{V}$$

The SI units for density are kg/m³. However, density is also commonly expressed in units of g/cm³ or g/mL. These are equivalent, because 1 cm³ = 1 mL. The density of water is exactly 1 g/cm³ (= 1 g/mL).

A *fluid* is any substance in which the particles that compose the substance are free to move past one another. This includes both liquids and gases. Whether or not a solid object will float in a fluid depends on the relative densities of the object and the fluid. If the object is denser than the fluid, the object will sink. If the object is less dense than the fluid, the object will float.

This is also true of two fluids in the same container. Unless the two fluids mix together, the fluid with less density will rise and the fluid with greater density will sink until the lighter fluid is floating on the denser fluid. For example, cooking oil has a density of about 0.91 g/mL, and it does not mix with water. If oil and water are put in the same container, the oil will float on top of the water.

The tendency for an object to float in a fluid is called *buoyancy*, and the upward force that a fluid exerts on a submerged or floating object is called **buoyant force**. Fluids always exert an upward force on submerged objects. The buoyant force of water is what makes objects that are underwater feel lighter than when they are in air. If the buoyant force is less than the weight of the object, the object will sink. If the buoyant force is greater than the object's weight, the object will rise until it is floating.

When an object is submerged in a fluid, the object takes up some of the space that was occupied by the fluid. In a liquid, you can observe this as you see the

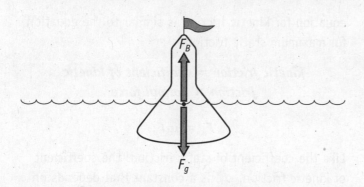

level of the liquid rise above the original level. The volume of this displaced fluid is equal to the volume of the submerged object (or of the part of the object that is submerged, if it is only partially submerged). You can find the mass of the displaced fluid from the density and volume of the displaced fluid:

**mass of displaced fluid =
density × displaced volume**

$$m_f = D \times V$$

The magnitude of the buoyant force is given by *Archimedes' principle*, which states:

The buoyant force of a fluid is equal to the weight of the displaced liquid.

This is expressed by the following equation:

$$F_B = m_f g$$

Note that Archimedes' principle applies to gases as well as liquids. However, because gases usually have low densities, the buoyant forces of gases are usually small. Archimedes' principle is used more often for liquids, such as water.

When an object is floating in a liquid, the buoyant force of the liquid equals the weight of the object, giving a net force of zero. A floating object is always partially submerged, however. The object is submerged to the point that the mass (and weight) of the displaced fluid equals the total mass (and weight) of the object.

Friction

Friction is a resistive force that opposes the relative motion of two surfaces in contact with one another. You experience and even depend on friction all the time. Friction is what allows your shoes to grip the sidewalk or a car's tires to grab the road. Friction helps keep a book, pencil, or glass of water from slipping out of your hand. Friction tends to dampen, or slow down, motion, and almost always causes an increase in temperature. Air resistance is also considered a type of friction.

When you are solving problems in physical science, you are often asked to "ignore friction" or "ignore air resistance." Ignoring friction often makes solving problems easier, but in the real world, friction is almost always present. So, it is important to understand and know how to solve problems involving friction to some degree. Friction in the real world is almost always complex and may depend on many factors, such as speed, direction, or temperature. However, in certain cases, such as when both surfaces are fairly smooth and dry, friction can be simplified to two basic types: static friction and kinetic friction.

Static friction is the friction between two surfaces that are at rest relative to one another. The magnitude of static friction actually changes depending on the other forces acting on an object. For example, imagine a heavy book on a table. Say you push on the book with a small horizontal force of 1 N. The book doesn't move, so you know the force of friction is equal and opposite to the force you have applied, making a net force of zero. Therefore, you know the force of static friction has a magnitude of 1 N. Now say you increase your force to 2 N, but the book still doesn't move. By the same reasoning, the static friction on the book now has a magnitude of 2 N.

Usually, the most interesting and relevant value of static friction is its maximum value. In the case of the book on the table, the maximum static friction would be equal in magnitude to the maximum force you could apply before the book started moving. The maximum static friction is calculated with the following equation:

**maximum static friction = coefficient of static
friction × normal force**

$$F_{s,max} = \mu_s F_n$$

The normal force, F_n, is simply the force of the surface on the object (for example, the upward force of the table on the book). The principle is the same as for the normal force on the box on a ramp discussed earlier. The coefficient of static friction, μ_s, is a constant that depends on the kind of materials the surfaces are made of. The coefficient of friction between metal and ice, for example, is small, while the coefficient of friction between metal and rubber is large. Coefficients of friction do not have units.

If you pushed hard enough on the book on the table, the book would start sliding across the table. Friction between two surfaces that are moving relative to one another is called **kinetic friction**. The equation for kinetic friction is similar to the equation for maximum static friction:

kinetic friction = coefficient of kinetic friction × normal force

$$F_k = \mu_k F_n$$

Like the coefficient of static friction, the coefficient of kinetic friction, μ_k, is a constant that depends on the kinds of materials that make up the surfaces. For any two given surfaces, the coefficient of kinetic friction is always less than the coefficient of static friction.

UNIT 3

Review

~~~~~~

Darken the circle by the correct answer.

1. Newton's first law is also called
   - Ⓐ the law of force.
   - Ⓑ the law of motion.
   - Ⓒ the law of inertia.
   - Ⓓ the law of momentum.

2. Which of the following expresses Newton's second law?
   - Ⓐ $p = mv$
   - Ⓑ $F_{net} = ma$
   - Ⓒ $F_g = G\,\dfrac{m_1 m_2}{r^2}$
   - Ⓓ $Ft = \Delta p$

3. Which of the following expresses Newton's third law?
   - Ⓐ Acceleration is always accompanied by a force.
   - Ⓑ Every action force is accompanied by an equal and opposite reaction force.
   - Ⓒ Objects tend to remain at rest or in motion at a constant speed.
   - Ⓓ The total momentum of an isolated system always remains constant.

4. What quantity measures the amount of matter in an object?
   - Ⓐ mass
   - Ⓑ weight
   - Ⓒ force
   - Ⓓ momentum

5. What is the SI unit for weight?
   - Ⓐ kg
   - Ⓑ lb
   - Ⓒ N
   - Ⓓ kg•m/s

6. Newton's law of universal gravitation can be applied
   - Ⓐ only to very massive objects.
   - Ⓑ only to objects in outer space.
   - Ⓒ only to objects near Earth's surface.
   - Ⓓ to any two objects with mass.

7. Centripetal force
   - Ⓐ causes centripetal acceleration.
   - Ⓑ is always a gravitational force.
   - Ⓒ is always either a gravitational force or a frictional force.
   - Ⓓ is parallel to an object's motion along a curved path.

8. If an object is floating in a liquid,
   - Ⓐ the density of the object equals the density of the liquid.
   - Ⓑ the mass of the submerged part of the object equals the mass of the displaced liquid.
   - Ⓒ the buoyant force on the object equals the object's weight.
   - Ⓓ the object has a greater density than the liquid.

Unit 3, Force
Physical Science, SV 0425-5

Review (cont'd.)

9. What kind of force opposes the relative motion of two contacting surfaces?

(A) normal force

(B) centripetal force

(C) gravitational force

(D) friction

10. Explain the difference between static friction and kinetic friction.

_____

_____

_____

Unit 3, Force
Physical Science, SV 0425-5

UNIT 3    Newton's Second Law

> Newton's second law expresses the relationship between the net force on an object and the object's acceleration:
>
> net force = mass × acceleration
>
> $F_{net} = ma$

Use Newton's second law to solve the following problems.

1. A 1520 kg car accelerates at a rate of 1.50 m/s². What is the net force on the car?

_____

2. A 5.22×10^7 kg cruise ship is moving at its top speed as it comes into port. The ship then undergoes an acceleration equal to −0.357 m/s² until it comes to rest at its anchorage. What is the net force acting on the ship as it slows down?

_____

3. A catcher in a professional baseball game exerts a force of −65.0 N to stop the ball. If the baseball has a mass of 0.145 kg, what is the ball's acceleration as it is being caught?

_____

4. A 214 kg boat is sinking in the ocean. The force of gravity that draws the boat downward is partially offset by the buoyant force of the water, so that the net force on the boat is −1310 N. What is the acceleration of the boat?

5. A freight train slows down as it approaches a train yard. If a force of -3.8×10^6 N is required to provide an acceleration of −0.33 m/s², what is the train's mass?

_____

6. A house is lifted from its foundations onto a truck for relocation. The net force lifting the house is 2850 N. This force causes the house to move from rest to an upward speed of 0.15 m/s in 5.0 s. What is the mass of the house?

_____

7. Because of a frictional force of 2.6 N, a force of 2.8 N must be applied to a textbook in order to slide it along the surface of a wooden table. The book accelerates at a rate of 0.11 m/s².

a. What is the net force on the book?

_____

b. What is the mass of the book?

_____

UNIT 3

Newton's Third Law

> *Newton's third law says that forces always occur in action-reaction pairs. The reaction force is equal in magnitude and opposite in direction to the action force.*

Fill in the blank to complete each action-reaction pair below.

Action

1. A bird's wings push air downward.

2. A car's tires push backward on the road.

3. _____

4. _____

5. A book pushes down on a table.

6. _____

Reaction

_____

_____

Fuel pushes the rocket upward.

Water pushes the dolphin forward.

_____

The bullet causes the gun to recoil.

7. Explain why a reaction force never cancels out the corresponding action force.

_____

_____

_____

_____

UNIT 3

Momentum and Impulse

> *An object's momentum is the product of the object's mass and its velocity:*
>
> $$p = mv$$
>
> *When a net force acts on an object for a period of time, the force causes a change in the object's momentum. This relationship is expressed in the impulse-momentum theorem:*
>
> $$Ft = \Delta p$$
>
> *The product Ft is called* **impulse***, and Δp refers to the change in momentum.*

Use the formulas to answer the questions.

1. Calculate the momentum of a high-speed "bullet train" with a mass of 9.2×10^8 kg moving at a speed of 61 m/s.

   _____

2. The brakes are engaged on the train in item 1. The brakes apply a frictional force of 6.4×10^8 N for 25 s. What is the change in the train's momentum?

   _____

3. What is the magnitude of the train's momentum after the brakes have been applied as in item 2?

   _____

4. How fast would a commercial jet airplane with a mass of 6.6×10^4 kg have to travel to have the same momentum as the train in item 1?

   _____

5. A pitcher in a professional baseball game throws a fastball, giving the baseball a momentum of 5.83 kg•m/s. If the baseball has a mass of 0.145 kg, what is the baseball's speed?

   _____

6. A batter hits the ball in item 5. What is the change in the ball's momentum if the ball returns to the pitcher with a momentum of −5.83 kg•m/s? (The momentum is negative because it is in the opposite direction from the pitch.)

   _____

7. What is the force of the bat on the ball in item 6 if the bat is in contact with the ball for 0.25 s?

   _____

UNIT 3

Force Diagrams

Use the information to draw the diagrams.

The force diagram at right shows the forces acting on a car when it is moving at a constant speed on a flat stretch of road. The normal force, F_n, is the upward force of the road on the car, and it is equal in magnitude to the car's weight, F_g. The forward force of the engine, F_e, is equal in magnitude to the force of friction, F_f. The force of friction may include both friction from the road and friction internal to the car, including friction due to application of the car's brakes. Because the net force on the car is zero, the car has no acceleration, positive or negative.

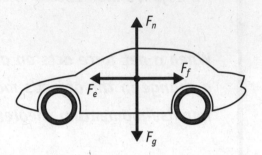

1. Draw a force diagram for the car when it is accelerating forward.

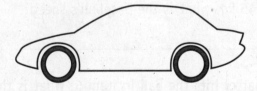

2. Draw a force diagram for the car when it is slowing down.

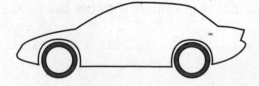

3. Draw a force diagram for the car when it is at rest (assume $F_e = 0$, as it would be in a car with a manual transmission).

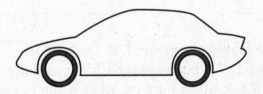

4. Draw a force diagram of the car moving at constant speed up a hill. Show components of the forces on an x–y axis system with the x-axis parallel to the road.

UNIT 3  Mass and Weight

> *Mass is an intrinsic property of an object, while weight is a force that depends on the value of the free-fall acceleration, g, at an object's location. Weight is related to mass in the following way:*
>
> $$weight = mass \times free\text{-}fall\ acceleration$$
> $$F_g = mg$$
>
> *Near Earth's surface, g = 9.81 m/s^2. On the surface of the moon, g = 1.63 m/s^2. The SI unit for mass is kilograms (kg). The SI unit for weight is newtons (N), while the British unit for weight is pounds of force (lb). 1 lb = 4.45 N.*

Answer the following questions about mass and weight.

An astronaut weighs herself on a scale on Earth. She finds that her weight, including her 180 lb space suit, is 315 lb. She then travels to the surface of the moon.

1. What is the astronaut's weight on Earth, in N? _____

2. What is the astronaut's mass on Earth (in kg)? _____

3. What is the astronaut's mass on the moon (in kg)? _____

4. What is the astronaut's weight on the moon, in N? _____

5. What is the astronaut's weight on the moon, in lb? _____

6. Starting with your weight in lb, calculate your weight in N and your mass in kg. Show all calculations.

Mass and Weight (cont'd.)

~~~~~~

7. Calculate what your weight would be on the moon, in both N and lb. Show your work.

8. Explain what is wrong with the following statement: "An astronaut in orbit experiences weightlessness."

_____

_____

_____

_____

UNIT 3    Forces in Orbital Motion

> Earth exerts a gravitational force on the moon in accordance with Newton's law of universal gravitation. This force acts as a centripetal force that holds the moon in a nearly circular orbit around Earth. The following are equations and data about forces in orbital motion.
>
> $$F_g = G\frac{m_1 m_2}{r^2} \qquad F_c = m\frac{v^2}{r}$$
>
> **Earth's mass:** $m_E = 5.97 \times 10^{24}$ kg   **moon's mass:** $m_M = 7.35 \times 10^{22}$ kg
>
> **Earth-moon distance:** $r = 3.84 \times 10^8$ m
>
> $G = 6.67 \times 10^{-11}$ N•m²/kg²

Use the equations and data to answer the following questions about the moon's orbit.

1. What is the magnitude of the gravitational force Earth exerts on the moon? _____

2. What is the magnitude of the centripetal force that holds the moon in its orbit? _____

3. What is the direction of the centripetal force on the moon? _____

4. What is the moon's speed along its orbit? (**Hint:** rearrange the equation for centripetal force to solve for *v*.) _____

Earth orbits the sun in a nearly circular orbit. The sun's mass is 1.99×10^{30} kg. The average distance from Earth to the sun is 1.50×10^{11} m.

5. What is the magnitude of the gravitational force the sun exerts on Earth? _____

6. What is the magnitude of the centripetal force that holds Earth in its orbit? _____

7. What is Earth's speed as it orbits the sun? _____

UNIT 3

Density

Density is a measurement of mass per unit volume. The equation for density is:

$$D = \frac{m}{V}$$

Water has a density of exactly 1 g/cm³ = 1 g/mL.

Answer the following questions about density.

1. What is the mass of 1 L of water?

   _____

2. Describe what will happen if a metal ball with a density of 2.3 g/cm³ is placed in water.

   _____

3. Cooking oil has a density of about 0.92 g/cm³. What will happen if oil and water are together in the same container?

   _____

4. Lithium is the lightest of metals and the least dense of all nongaseous elements. A pure lithium sample with a volume of 13.0 cm³ has a mass of 6.94 g. What is the density of lithium?

   _____

5. The largest meteorite discovered on Earth is the Hoba West stone in Namibia, Africa. The volume of the meteorite is about 7.5 m³. If the stone has a density of 8.0 × 10³ kg/m³, what is the mass of the meteorite?

   _____

6. One of the largest emeralds ever discovered had a mass of 17.23 kg. If the density of the emerald was 4.02 g/cm³, what was the emerald's volume?

   _____

7. Outer space is often described as a vacuum, but there is always some matter present. In the space 300 km above Earth's surface, there is as little as 1.58 × 10⁻¹² g of matter in a 500.0 cm³ volume of space. Based on this data, what is the density of the matter in space?

   _____

8. The density of the material in a neutron star is similar to the density inside the nucleus of an atom, abot 2 × 10¹⁴ g/cm³. If a teaspoon has a volume of 4.9 cm³, what would be the mass of a teaspoon of the material from a neutron star?

   _____

Unit 3, Force
Physical Science, SV 0425-5

UNIT 3

Buoyancy

> **Buoyant force is the upward force a fluid exerts on a submerged or partially submerged object. Buoyant force is equal to the weight of the fluid displaced by the object:**
>
> $$F_B = m_f g$$
>
> **If an object is floating, the buoyant force also equals the weight of the object.**

Answer the following questions about buoyancy.

A beach ball with an average density of 1.3 kg/m^3 and a volume of 3.4×10^{-2} m^3 is held in place at the bottom of a swimming pool.

1. What is the mass of the ball? _____

2. What is the weight of the ball? _____

3. What volume of water does the ball displace? _____

4. What is the mass of the displaced water? ($D = 1000$ kg/m^3) _____

5. What is the weight of the displaced water? _____

6. What is the magnitude of the buoyant force on the ball? _____

The beach ball is released, accelerates toward the surface of the water, pops out of the water, and finally comes to rest floating at the water's surface.

7. What is the net force on the ball when it is floating at rest? _____

8. What is the magnitude of the buoyant force on the floating ball? _____

UNIT 3

Friction

Friction is a force that opposes the relative motion between two surfaces that are in contact. Friction can be calculated fairly simply for dry, smooth, solid surfaces. Maximum static friction, $F_{s,max}$, is the friction that must be overcome to start an object moving from rest. Kinetic friction, F_k, is the force of friction between surfaces in relative motion.

$$F_{s,max} = \mu_s F_n \qquad\qquad F_k = \mu_k F_n$$

μ_s is the coefficient of static friction, while μ_k is the coefficient of kinetic friction. These coefficients do not have units. F_n is the normal force, which is perpendicular to the surface of contact.

Answer the following questions about friction.

A book with a mass of 0.45 kg is resting on a flat, smooth table. The coefficient of static friction between the book and the table is 0.62, while the coefficient of kinetic friction is 0.51.

1. What is the weight of the book? _____

2. What is the magnitude of the normal force on the book? _____

3. What is the maximum force of static friction on the book? _____

4. What is the minimum force you can exert on the book to get it to start sliding across the table? _____

5. What is the force of kinetic friction on the book once it is moving? _____

6. If you push on the book with the force you found in item 4, what is the book's acceleration? _____

One end of the table is lifted so that the surface of the table is at an angle of 30° above the horizontal.

7. What is the magnitude of the normal force on the book? _____

8. What is the maximum force of static friction on the book? _____

9. What is the magnitude of the component of the book's weight that is parallel to the tabletop? _____

10. What is the force of kinetic friction on the book in motion? _____

11. Will the book start sliding on its own, or does it still need a push? Explain your answer.

_____

_____

_____

UNIT 3

Force Crossword

ACROSS

2. Same as the force of gravity

4. Depends on mass and distance

9. Constant used in calculating friction

10. The tendency to resist acceleration

11. The cause of acceleration

DOWN

1. The units of force

3. A resistive force between two surfaces that are in contact

5. Mass per unit volume

6. Mass times velocity

7. Accompanies an action force

8. The upward force of a fluid

Newton's laws and the principles of force are one set of tools for understanding the behavior of physical systems. Another useful set of tools involves the principles of **energy**. Energy can be defined broadly as the ability to move or change matter.

Matter and energy are the two most fundamental components of our universe. Some people debate whether energy is a *substance*, on par with matter, or if energy is just an abstract quantity, like acceleration or momentum. As it turns out, matter can turn into energy, and vice-versa, so many scientists now believe there is really only one fundamental substance, which can either take the form of matter or of energy.

However, the philosophical debate about the true nature of energy is not our primary interest here. We want to use the principles of energy to understand how the physical world works and to solve problems in the realm of physical science. In many cases, approaching a problem in terms of energy can be much simpler than approaching the same problem in terms of force.

Key Terms

energy—the ability to move or change matter

kinetic energy (KE)—energy associated with an object due to the object's motion

potential energy (PE)—energy that is stored within a system

elastic potential energy—energy stored in a stretched or compressed medium

gravitational potential energy (PE_g)—potential energy due to an object's position in a gravitational field

work (W)—energy transferred by a force; a quantity equal to the product of the force on an object and the distance the object moves

thermal energy—the total kinetic energy of particles within an object or substance

chemical potential energy—energy stored in the chemical bonds that bind atoms to one another

nuclear energy—energy that binds protons and neutrons together inside the nucleus of an atom

electrical energy—energy associated with charged particles

power (P)—the rate at which energy is transferred

simple machine—a simple device that redistributes force when doing work

compound machine—a device composed of two or more simple machines

mechanical advantage (MA)—the ratio of the output force to the input force in a machine

efficiency—the ratio of useful work output to work input in a machine

Kinetic Energy

Energy can take many different forms. However, all the different forms of energy can be divided into two categories: kinetic energy and potential energy.

Kinetic energy is the energy associated with a moving object due to the object's motion. Kinetic energy is calculated with the following equation:

$$kinetic\ energy = \frac{1}{2} \times mass \times velocity^2$$

$$KE = \frac{1}{2}mv^2$$

From the equation, you might guess that the units for kinetic energy are $kg \cdot m^2/s^2$. These units are equivalent to the standard SI units for energy: joules (J). Note that energy, in any of its forms, is not a vector. It has only a magnitude, not a direction.

Potential Energy

Potential energy is energy that is stored in a system. For example, **elastic potential energy** is energy stored in a stretched or compressed object. When an archer holds a bow with the arrow ready to launch, both the string and the body of the bow are stretched. The bow and arrow system has elastic potential energy. This energy is stored until the bow is released; after the bow is released, the elastic potential energy in the bow is transferred to the arrow, giving it kinetic energy.

Another common form of potential energy is **gravitational potential energy**. Near Earth's surface, gravitational potential energy depends on the position of an object relative to Earth's surface—in other words, the object's height. Gravitational potential energy also depends on the mass of the object and the free-fall acceleration, g:

$$gravitational\ PE = mass \times g \times height$$

$$PE_g = mgh$$

Note that gravitational potential energy, like kinetic energy, has units of $kg \cdot m^2/s^2$. Again, these units are equivalent to the standard SI units for energy: joules (J).

Work

Work is energy transferred by the action of a force. Quantitatively, work is calculated as the product of the force on an object and the distance the object moves:

$$work = force \times distance$$

$$W = Fd$$

Work has SI units of N•m or J. You may recall that $1\ N = 1\ kg \cdot m/s^2$. An analysis of units shows that a N•m is equivalent to a J:

$$1\ N \bullet m = (1\ kg \bullet m/s^2) \times (1\ m) = 1\ kg \bullet m^2/s^2 = 1\ J$$

Note that if a force is applied to an object, but the object doesn't move, then no work is done. In this way, the scientific meaning of *work* differs from the everyday usage of the word. If you hold a heavy book at arm's length for an extended period of time, you may feel like you are doing a lot of work, but according to the scientific definition of work, you are not doing any work on the book; the distance the book moves is zero, and no energy is transferred to the book in the process. You *are*, however, doing work at the cellular level, in the muscles of your arms.

When a net force does net work on an object, the kinetic energy of the object changes. This is expressed mathematically in the *work-kinetic energy theorem*:

$$net\ work = change\ in\ kinetic\ energy$$

$$W_{net} = \Delta KE$$

For example, if the net force on a car is 250 N as the car moves a distance of 20 m, the net work done on the car is 5000 J:

$$W_{net} = F_{net}d = (250\ N)(20\ m) = 5000\ N \bullet m = 5000\ J$$

According to the work-kinetic energy theorem, the increase in the kinetic energy of the car is also 5000 J.

Other Forms of Energy

The kinetic and potential energy in systems at the macroscopic level, that is, at scales we can observe directly, are sometimes called *mechanical energy*. However, kinetic and potential energy also exist at

Unit 4, Energy
Physical Science, SV 0425-5

the molecular level, that is, at the level of atoms and molecules. Energy at the molecular level of a system is sometimes referred to as *nonmechanical energy*.

One example of energy at the molecular level is the kinetic energy of particles as they jostle and move about inside an object. This energy is called **thermal energy**, or sometimes *internal energy*.

Another form of energy at the molecular level is the potential energy stored in the chemical bonds that bind atoms to one another. This energy is sometimes called **chemical potential energy**. Changes in chemical potential energy only take place when chemical reactions occur.

Nuclear energy is found at an even smaller scale. Nuclear energy is the energy that binds protons and neutrons together inside the nucleus of an atom. Nuclear energy is a form of potential energy that can be released in a nuclear event such as fission, fusion, or nuclear decay. In nuclear reactions, small amounts of matter can be converted into large amounts of energy.

Electrical energy is the energy associated with charged particles, such as electrons or ions (atoms with a net charge). Electrical energy can be kinetic or potential.

Sound and light can also be considered forms of energy. Sound carries energy through a medium, such as air or water, in the form of sound waves. Light can carry energy through a medium or through a vacuum.

Conservation of Energy

We have already discussed some of the many different forms of energy. Although each of these types is distinct conceptually, energy often changes from one form to another. In fact, most physical processes involve some form of energy transformation. However, although energy often changes form, the total amount of energy in a closed system doesn't change. This is known as the *law of conservation of energy*. Another way of stating this law is:

Energy is neither created nor destroyed, although it may change form.

Let's consider a simple example. If you toss a ball straight up into the air, the ball leaves your hand with a certain amount of kinetic energy. As the ball

rises, this kinetic energy is transformed into potential energy. You know the kinetic energy is decreasing because the speed of the ball is decreasing. You also know the gravitational potential energy is increasing because the ball's height is increasing. When the ball reaches its peak height, all the energy is potential energy. The kinetic energy at that point is zero because the ball's speed is zero. Because energy is conserved, you know that the potential energy at that point is equal to the initial kinetic energy of the ball when you first released it.

As the ball starts to fall back down, potential energy is transformed back into kinetic energy. By the time the ball reaches your hand again, all of the potential energy that was gained has been lost again, while all of the kinetic energy that was lost has been regained. As a result, the speed of the ball when you catch it is the same as it was when you first released it. Throughout the whole process, the total energy remains the same, although the energy is continually changing form.

Note that mechanical energy—kinetic and potential energy at the macroscopic level—is only conserved in ideal systems where there is no friction. However, friction is present in most physical processes in the real world. When friction is present, mechanical energy may not be conserved, but the total energy is still conserved. This is possible because some of the mechanical energy is transformed into other forms of energy, such as thermal energy or sound.

For example, consider again the example of tossing a ball into the air. If you take into account air resistance (a form of friction), then you know that the speed of the ball when it returns to your hand will be slightly less than it was when you first released the ball. It might seem, therefore, that some energy has been lost or destroyed. The "missing" energy has not truly been lost, however; it has been transformed into other forms of energy—in this case, mostly into thermal energy. If you were able to measure the temperature of the ball and the air both before and after the toss, and to great precision, you would find that the temperature of both the ball and the air increased slightly as a result of this transformation of mechanical energy to thermal energy.

Whenever kinetic friction is present, some kinetic energy will be transformed into thermal energy. In situations that involve transformations to or from elastic potential energy, some energy will be transformed into sound as well. For example, when you drop a tennis ball, it doesn't quite reach its initial height when it bounces back up. Some of the "missing" energy in this case has been transformed into sound—producing the sound you hear when the ball hits the ground.

Power

Power is the rate at which energy is transferred. If energy is transferred by a force doing work on an object, power is the rate at which that work is done:

$$power = \frac{work}{time}$$

$$P = \frac{W}{t}$$

The SI units for power are watts (W). 1 W is equivalent to 1 J/s. In other words, a watt describes energy transfer at a rate of one joule every second.

For example, if the engine of a car does 7500 J of work on the car—that is, increases the car's kinetic energy by 7500 J—in 10 s, then the average power output of the engine during that time is 750 W:

$$P = \frac{W}{t} = \frac{7500 \text{ J}}{10 \text{ s}} = 750 \text{ J/s} = 750 \text{ W}$$

Another common unit of power, especially in engines, is horsepower (hp). 1 hp = 746 W.

Simple Machines

A **simple machine** is a simple device that helps people do work. Most simple machines make doing work easier by changing the amount of force required to do the work, with a corresponding change to the distance over which the force is applied. The six basic types of simple machines are the lever, the pulley, the wheel and axle, the inclined plane, the wedge, and the screw.

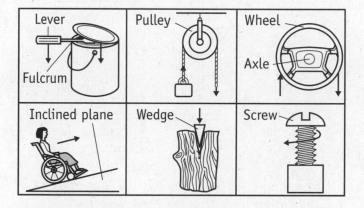

The *input force* is the amount of force applied to a machine, and the *output force* is the amount of force the machine applies to do the desired work. The *input distance* and the *output distance* are the respective distances over which these forces are applied. The input force on a machine is sometimes called the *effort*, and the output force is sometimes called the *load*.

A lever is a rigid rod, or *lever arm*, that rotates about a fixed point called the *fulcrum*. If you use a screwdriver to pry the lid off a can of paint, you are using the screwdriver as a lever. The fulcrum is the pivoting point where the screwdriver rests on the edge of the can. Your hand applies an input force to the handle of the screwdriver, and the handle moves through a certain input distance. At the same time, the tip of the screwdriver moves through a much smaller output distance, but applies a much larger output force to the lid on the paint can.

There are three classes of levers. In a first-class lever, the fulcrum lies between the input force and the output force. A playground see-saw is an example of a first-class lever. The screwdriver in the example above is also a first-class lever.

First-class lever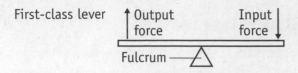

In a second-class lever, the fulcrum is at one end and the input force is at the other end. A wheelbarrow is an example of a second-class lever.

Second-class lever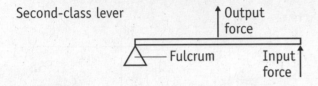

Third-class lever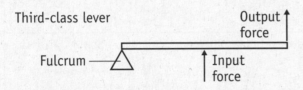

In a third-class lever, the fulcrum is at one end and the output force is at the other end; the input force acts between the fulcrum and the output force. This class of levers has a smaller output force than input force. When you use a broom to sweep a floor, the broom is acting as a third-class lever.

A pulley is a wheel with a string or rope threaded around it. Using a single pulley does not multiply force, but simply redirects force. However, threading a rope through multiple pulleys can increase input distance, and thereby multiply the output force.

A wheel and axle is essentially a pulley or a lever attached to a central shaft. A steering wheel is an example of a wheel and axle, as is a screwdriver used to drive in a screw.

A wheelchair ramp is an example of an inclined plane. Inclined planes make work easier by increasing the distance over which force is applied, making the required input force less.

A wedge is essentially two inclined planes back-to-back. Wedges are used to multiply and redirect forces to push two surfaces apart.

A screw is an inclined plane wrapped around a shaft. Like inclined planes, screws reduce the required

input force by increasing the distance over which force is applied.

A **compound machine** is a device composed of one or more simple machines. For example, a pair of scissors is made of two levers joined at a fulcrum; one side of each of these levers is also a wedge that can cut into a piece of paper.

Mechanical Advantage

Using a lever to pry open a paint can is much easier than trying to open the can directly with your fingers. This is because the amount of input force required is less when using a lever. However, using a simple machine does not change the total amount of work done. Under ideal conditions, in which mechanical energy is conserved, the output work of a simple machine equals the input work:

$$output\ work = input\ work$$

$$W_{out} = W_{in}$$

Rewriting this using the definition of work gives the following:

$$output\ force \times output\ distance = input\ force \times input\ distance$$

$$F_{out}d_{out} = F_{in}d_{in}$$

We can rearrange this equation again to get the following:

$$\frac{F_{out}}{F_{in}} = \frac{d_{in}}{d_{out}}$$

The ratio found on each side of this equation is referred to as the **mechanical advantage** of a machine. The mechanical advantage tells you how much the machine multiplies force.

As stated above, the input force on a machine is sometimes called the *effort*, and the output force is sometimes called the *load*. Mechanical advantage can therefore be calculated with any of the following ratios:

$$MA = \frac{load}{effort} = \frac{F_{out}}{F_{in}} = \frac{d_{in}}{d_{out}}$$

Efficiency

The output work of a machine equals the input work under ideal conditions. However, in the real world, ideal conditions are never met completely. As a result, the output of useful work—work that the machine is intended to do—is actually always less than the work put into the machine:

$$W_{out} < W_{in}$$

The relationship between the input work and the output of useful work by a machine is expressed in a ratio called **efficiency**:

$$efficiency = \frac{useful\ work\ output}{work\ input}$$

$$eff = \frac{W_{out}}{W_{in}}$$

Efficiency is often expressed as a percentage. To turn a ratio into a percentage, just multiply the ratio by 100 and add a percent sign (%). The efficiency of an ideal machine, in which friction was completely absent, would be 100%. All real machines have efficiencies somewhat less than 100%.

UNIT 4

Review

Darken the circle by the correct answer.

1. Which of the following has units of joules (J)?

Ⓐ kinetic energy

Ⓑ potential energy

Ⓒ work

Ⓓ All of the above

2. What kind of energy is associated with an object due to the object's motion?

Ⓐ kinetic energy

Ⓑ potential energy

Ⓒ mechanical energy

Ⓓ power

3. If the speed of an object doubles, the kinetic energy of the object

Ⓐ doubles.

Ⓑ is reduced by half.

Ⓒ is multiplied by 4.

Ⓓ does not change.

4. Which of the following is the correct equation for calculating gravitational potential energy?

Ⓐ $PE_g = \frac{1}{2} mgh$

Ⓑ $PE_g = mgh$

Ⓒ $PE_g = mv^2$

Ⓓ $PE_g = \frac{1}{2} mv^2$

5. When an archer releases a bow,

Ⓐ kinetic energy is transformed into potential energy.

Ⓑ potential energy is transformed into kinetic energy.

Ⓒ elastic potential energy is transformed into gravitational potential energy.

Ⓓ gravitational potential energy is transformed into elastic potential energy.

6. If a force is applied to an object, but the object doesn't move,

Ⓐ the work done on the object is positive.

Ⓑ the work done on the object is negative.

Ⓒ the work done on the object depends on the magnitude and direction of the force.

Ⓓ no work is done on the object.

7. The law of conservation of energy states that

Ⓐ energy always leaks out of a system.

Ⓑ energy never leaks out of a system.

Ⓒ energy cannot be created or destroyed.

Ⓓ mechanical energy is always conserved.

8. Friction commonly causes

Ⓐ kinetic energy to be converted into potential energy.

Ⓑ potential energy to be converted into kinetic energy.

Ⓒ kinetic energy to be converted into thermal energy.

Ⓓ potential energy to be converted into sound.

9. The rate at which energy is transferred is called

   (A) work.

   (B) power.

   (C) mechanical advantage.

   (D) efficiency.

10. List the six types of simple machines and an example of each.

_____

_____

_____

_____

_____

UNIT 4

Kinetic Energy

> *Kinetic energy is the energy associated with a moving object. The equation for calculating kinetic energy is:*
>
> $$\text{kinetic energy} = \frac{1}{2} \times \text{mass} \times \text{velocity}^2 \qquad KE = \frac{1}{2}mv^2$$

Use the equation for kinetic energy to solve the following problems.

1. A cheetah can run briefly with a speed of 31 m/s. Suppose a cheetah with a mass of 47 kg runs at this speed. What is the cheetah's kinetic energy?

_____

2. A table tennis ball has a mass of about 2.45 g. Suppose the ball is hit across the table with a speed of 4.0 m/s. What is the ball's kinetic energy?

_____

3. A baseball traveling at a speed of 35 m/s has 89 J of kinetic energy. What is the mass of the baseball?

_____

4. A meteoroid entering Earth's atmosphere has a speed of 70.0 km/s and a kinetic energy of 2.56×10^{15} J. What is the mass of the meteoroid?

_____

5. The kinetic energy of a golf ball is measured to be 143 J. If the golf ball has a mass of 47 g, what is its speed? (Hint: Rearrange the equation for kinetic energy to solve for *v*. The equation will involve a square root.)

_____

6. When a 65 kg skydiver jumps from a plane, her speed steadily increases until air resistance provides a force that balances the force due to free fall. How fast is the skydiver falling if her kinetic energy is 7.0×10^5 J?

_____

7. A 725 kg car has a kinetic energy of 302 kJ as it travels along a highway. What is the car's speed?

_____

UNIT 4  Gravitational Potential Energy

> Near Earth's surface, gravitational potential energy depends on an object's mass and height, and on the free-fall acceleration, g:
>
> gravitational PE = mass × g × height $PE_g = mgh$

Use the equation for gravitational potential energy to solve the following problems.

1. What is the gravitational potential energy associated with a 75 kg tourist at the top floor of the Sears Tower in Chicago, with respect to the street 436 m below?

   _____

2. An Olympic diver weighing 650 N is on a platform 10 m above the water. What is the diver's gravitational potential energy with respect to the water? (Hint: $F_g = mg$.)

   _____

3. A bird carries a 25 g oyster to a height of 11 m. What is the gravitational potential energy of the oyster?

   _____

4. The bird from problem 3 drops the oyster. As it falls, all of the gravitational potential energy is transformed into kinetic energy (air resistance is negligible). What is the speed of the oyster when it hits the ground? ($KE = \frac{1}{2}mv^2$)

5. The world record for pole vaulting is 6.15 m. If the pole vaulter's gravitational potential at his maximum height was 4942 J, what was his mass?

   _____

6. An automobile to be transported by ship is raised 7.0 m above the dock. If its gravitational potential energy is 6.6×10^4 J, what is the automobile's mass?

   _____

7. An Olympic high-jumper with a mass of 82.0 kg has a gravitational potential energy of 1970 J at the peak height of the jump. How high is the jump?

   _____

8. A 1750 kg weather satellite moves in a circular orbit with a gravitational potential energy of 1.69×10^{10} J with respect to Earth's surface. At its location, free-fall acceleration is only 6.44 m/s². How high above Earth's surface is the satellite?

   _____

UNIT 4    Work

> **Work is energy transferred by the action of a force. Work is calculated as the product of the force on an object and the distance the object moves:**
>
> work = force × distance $W = Fd$
>
> **The work-kinetic energy theorem states that the net work done on an object equals the change in the object's kinetic energy:**
>
> net work = change in kinetic energy $W_{net} = \Delta KE$

Answer the following questions.

1. An old house is being lifted by a type of crane from its foundation and moved by truck to another location. If the house, which weighs 1.5×10^4 N, is lifted 1.52 m from the foundation to the bed of the truck, what is the minimum amount of work done by the crane on the house?

_____

2. After the house in problem 1 has been set on the truck bed, the truck accelerates until it reaches a constant speed. If the net force on the house is 3150 N and the truck moves a distance of 75.5 m while accelerating, how much net work is done on the house?

_____

3. What is the change in the kinetic energy of the house as a result of the work done in problem 2? _____

4. A child pulls a sled up a snow-covered hill. In the process, the child does 405 J of work on the sled. If she walks a distance of 15 m up the hill, how large a force does she exert on the sled?

_____

5. A car has run out of gas. Fortunately, there is a gas station nearby. You must exert a force of 715 N on the car in order to move it. By the time you reach the station, you have done 2.72×10^4 J of work on the car. How far have you pushed the car? _____

6. The kinetic energy of a book increases from 0 J to 2.7 J as you push the book across a table. What is the net work done on the book?

_____

7. If the force of friction did −1.2 J of work on the book in problem 6, how much work did you do on the book? _____

UNIT 4

Conservation of Energy in a Simple Pendulum

A simple pendulum consists of a relatively heavy mass, called a "pendulum bob," hanging from a string. When the pendulum bob is pushed or pulled to the side, the pendulum is displaced from its resting position. The pendulum then starts to swing back and forth in a regular, repeated motion. A simple pendulum is a classic system for studying the conservation of energy.

Consider the pendulum shown in the diagram at right. The pendulum bob has a mass of 0.25 kg. The pendulum bob is pulled to the right so that its height is 0.35 m vertically above the center position, and is then released. Assume for now that frictional forces are negligible, so that mechanical energy will be conserved in this system.

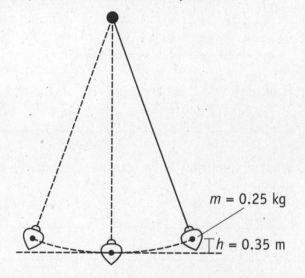

$m = 0.25$ kg

$h = 0.35$ m

1. What is the gravitational potential energy of the pendulum bob—relative to its normal center position—when it is first released?

_____

2. What is the kinetic energy of the pendulum bob when it is first released?

_____

3. Describe the energy transformation that takes place as the pendulum swings from its maximum displacement back toward the center position.

_____

4. What is the gravitational potential energy of the pendulum bob as it passes through the center position?

_____

5. What is the kinetic energy of the pendulum bob as it passes through the center position?

_____

6. What is the speed of the pendulum bob as it passes through the center position?

(Hint: Rearrange $KE = \frac{1}{2} mv^2$ to solve for v, and use the KE from problem 5.)

_____

Conservation of Energy in a Simple Pendulum (cont'd.)

7. Describe the energy transformation that takes place as the pendulum swings from the center position toward its maximum displacement on the left side of its swing.

   _____

   _____

8. How high will the pendulum rise on the left side of its swing?

   _____

9. What assumption have you made about the total energy of the system while making these predictions?

   _____

   _____

10. In a real pendulum, frictional forces are not completely negligible. A swinging pendulum will slow down over time and eventually stop. Does this mean a real pendulum violates the law of conservation of energy? Explain your answer.

   _____

   _____

   _____

UNIT 4

Power

> If energy is transferred by a force doing work on an object, power is the rate at which that work is done:
>
> $$power = \frac{work}{time} \qquad P = \frac{W}{t}$$
>
> The SI units for power are watts (W).

Answer the following questions about power.

1. A car engine does 1.25×10^5 J of work in 25 s. What is the power output of the engine?

_____

2. A space shuttle is placed in orbit by three engines that do 6.1×10^9 J of work in 8.5 min. What is the power output of these engines?

_____

3. A steam turbine is designed to be used as a power generator. The turbine provides enough power to do 3×10^{10} J of work in 1 min. What is the power output of the turbine?

_____

4. A certain tugboat can provide a maximum of 8.17×10^6 W of power. How much work can the tugboat do in 12.0 s?

_____

5. One horsepower (1 hp) is a unit of power based on the work that a horse can do in one second. 1 hp equals 746 W. Suppose you have a horse that has a power output of 750 W. How much work does this horse do in 0.55 s?

_____

6. Suppose a weightlifter's power output is 356 W during the time he does 3310 J of work on the weights. How long does it take the weightlifter to raise the weights?

_____

7. An icebreaker is a ship designed to break through ice, for example, in Arctic waters. One powerful icebreaker is powered by a nuclear reactor with a power output of 56 MW (5.6×10^7 W). How long does it take for this reactor to do 5.35×10^{10} J of work?

_____

UNIT 4

Simple Machines

Label each of the simple machines.

1. _____ 2. _____ 3. _____

4. _____ 5. _____ 6. _____

7. Draw a diagram of a first-class lever. Show the locations of the fulcrum, the input force (effort), and the output force (load).

8. Give an example of a first-class lever.

Simple Machines (cont'd.)

9. Draw a diagram of a second-class lever. Show the locations of the fulcrum, the input force (effort), and the output force (load).

10. Give an example of a second-class lever.

_____

11. Draw a diagram of a third-class lever. Show the locations of the fulcrum, the input force (effort), and the output force (load).

12. Give an example of a third-class lever.

_____

13. A bicycle is a compound machine. List three simple machines that can be found on a bicycle.

_____

_____

UNIT 4    Mechanical Advantage

---

Mechanical advantage is a measurement of how much a machine multiplies force. Mechanical advantage can be calculated as follows:

$$MA = \frac{load}{effort} = \frac{F_{out}}{F_{in}}$$

In an ideal machine with no friction, mechanical advantage is also equal to $\frac{d_{in}}{d_{out}}$.

Answer the following questions.

1. A system of pulleys is used to raise a heavy crate. The pulley system is such that an input force of 223 N is needed to provide an output force of 1784 N. What is the mechanical advantage of this pulley system?

_____

2. A mover uses a ramp to load a crate of nails onto a truck. The crate, which must be lifted 1.4 m from the street to the bed of the truck, is pushed along the length of the ramp. There are rollers along the ramp that make the friction between the crate and the ramp negligible. If the ramp is 4.6 m long, what is the mechanical advantage of the ramp?

_____

3. A wedge with a mechanical advantage of 4.2 is used to raise a house corner from its foundation. If the output force is 7500 N, what is the input force?

_____

4. The mechanical advantage of a wheel and axle is 8.50. If the output force that turns the axle is 2.22×10^3 N, what is the input force on the wheel?

_____

5. A lever and fulcrum are used to raise a heavy rock, which has a weight of 445 N. If the lever has a mechanical advantage of 9.50, what must the input force on the lever be in order to lift the rock?

_____

6. If the input force on the lever in problem 5 is 135 N, what is the net force on the rock?

_____

7. Explain why it is impossible for an inclined plane to have a mechanical advantage less than one (when friction is ignored).

_____

_____

_____

UNIT 4

Efficiency

> **Efficiency is a ratio or percentage that expresses the relationship between the input work and the output work in a machine:**
>
> $$\text{efficiency} = \frac{\text{work output}}{\text{work input}}$$
>
> $$eff = \frac{W_{out}}{W_{in}}$$

Answer the following questions about efficiency.

1. An inclined plane allows you to do 280 J of useful work on a refrigerator that you are sliding upward along the plane. If the work that you have to do is 760 J, what is the efficiency of the plane?

_____

2. The motor in a forklift uses 7.6×10^6 J of energy to do 1.8×10^6 J of work in lifting a heavy load. What is the efficiency of the forklift?

_____

3. 808 J of work are done on a car jack with an efficiency of 0.625. What is the useful work output of the jack?

_____

4. How much useful work can be done by a diesel engine with an efficiency of 0.39 if the work done on the pistons in the engine is 750 kJ?

_____

5. A gasoline engine does 225 J of useful work with each stroke of its pistons. If the engine has an efficiency of 29.0 percent, what is the amount of work done on the pistons in the engine?

_____

6. A system of pulleys does 1.25×10^5 J of useful work, but friction limits the system to an efficiency of 0.45. What is the amount of work that must be done on the pulleys?

_____

7. What conditions are required for the efficiency of a machine to be 100%?

_____

_____

_____

UNIT 4

Energy Word Find

Find the answers to the following in the word find puzzle below.

```
B F K P H Q A H Q K W L N Y E E
P U N A W A B V X R Y V S N S W
W Z T X L A S M V G V F I Y G Z
U K Q Y G Q T M V W G H Y D M R
P P R G Z W V T U E C P N L Y F
Q P B Y O D Y T J A N T G G T U
T U D R K Q R P M F O Y O B R L
O Y K I R E Y D G M C C C X R C
T H Y O G N N B J N Y F O A P R
X P F G A U L O E Z J A G K Y U
N A U D O E U I I H S R X J B M
K R K P O L C R E W O P S Q T S
W N M U E I A A T Y E I D A P O
D O Q D F B N T P M Y E B A N K
C E Q F D M E C H A N I C A L C
H A E D F V T S W V W B G P P M
```

1. The SI unit of energy

_____

2. Describes kinetic and potential energy at the macroscopic level

_____

3. Equal to force times distance

_____

4. The rate at which energy is transferred

_____

5. The SI unit of power

_____

6. The pivot point of a lever

_____

7. Made of more than one simple machine

_____

8. The ratio of useful work output to work input

_____

In the unit on energy, we focused primarily on forms of energy at the macroscopic level—in systems at the level we can observe directly. We also touched briefly on other forms of energy that exist at the microscopic level—the level of atoms and molecules. In this unit, we will continue to discuss energy, but our focus will now be on the energy at the microscopic level. As we shift to the microscopic view, you will have to use your imagination to visualize the physical events that are taking place.

Most matter in the universe is composed of atoms or molecules. These tiny particles are constantly in motion. In gases, the particles can be thought of as independent from each other, like tiny billiard balls flying around and occasionally bouncing off each other. In solids, the particles are bound to each other, so they are more likely to vibrate in place than to move over large distances. In liquids, the situation is somewhat in between gases and solids. The particles in a liquid are loosely bound, as if they are kind of sticky, and they may slide past each other as well as vibrate and rotate.

Recall that **kinetic energy** is the energy associated with an object due to its motion. As the particles that make up an object or a substance move—whether they are moving in a straight line, rotating, or vibrating in place—they have kinetic energy. The total kinetic energy of these particles

Key Terms

kinetic energy (KE)—energy associated with an object due to the object's motion

thermal energy (U)—the total kinetic energy of particles within an object or substance

temperature (T)—a measure of the average kinetic energy of particles within an object or substance

work (W)—energy transferred by a force; a quantity equal to the product of the force on an object and the distance the object moves

heat (Q)—energy transferred at the atomic level due to a temperature difference

conduction—the transfer of energy as heat between two objects in direct contact

convection—the transfer of energy by the movement of fluids with different temperatures

radiation—the transfer of energy by electromagnetic waves

specific heat (c)—the amount of energy required to raise the temperature of 1 kg of a substance by 1 degree (1 K or 1°C)

latent heat (L)—the energy per unit mass required for a substance to complete a phase change

heat engine—a device that converts heat or thermal energy to useful mechanical energy

thermodynamics—the scientific study of the relationship between heat and other forms of energy

entropy—a measure of the disorder in a system

within an object or substance is called **thermal energy**, or sometimes *internal energy*. In either case, the symbol for this kind of energy is *U*.

Temperature

If you wanted to quantify the thermal energy in an object, you would probably start by measuring **temperature**. Temperature is a measure of the *average* kinetic energy of particles within an object or substance.

A device that measures temperature is called a *thermometer*. The most common thermometers rely on *thermal expansion*—the expansion of a substance due to an increase in temperature. These thermometers usually contain a liquid, either mercury or colored alcohol, in a narrow column. As the temperature of the thermometer increases, the liquid expands, and the height of the column increases. The temperature is then measured by comparing the height of the column to a scale on the thermometer.

The temperature scale most widely used throughout the world is the Celsius scale. On the Celsius scale, 0°C is defined as the temperature of a mixture of water and ice at normal atmospheric pressure (essentially the freezing point of water), and 100°C is defined as the temperature of a mixture of water and steam (essentially the boiling point of water), also at normal atmospheric pressure. In the U.S. and U.K., we often use the Fahrenheit scale for measuring temperature. On the Fahrenheit scale, the freezing point of water is 32°F and the boiling point of water is 212°F.

You can convert temperatures between these two scales using the following equations:

Fahrenheit to Celsius: $T_C = \dfrac{5}{9}(T_F - 32.0)$

Celsius to Fahrenheit: $T_F = \dfrac{9}{5}T_C + 32.0$

The units within each of these scales, either °F or °C, are found by evenly dividing the scale between the 0 and 100 points. Note that a degree on the Celsius scale is not equivalent to a degree on the Fahrenheit scale.

The SI units for temperature are neither °F or °C; they are kelvins (K). 0 K is defined as the temperature of a substance in a theoretical state in which the particles have no kinetic energy at all. This temperature is also called *absolute zero*. On the Celsius scale, this theoretical temperature would be −273.15°C. A kelvin is equivalent to a degree on the Celsius scale, so converting between the Kelvin scale and the Celsius scale involves simply adding or subtracting 273.15:

Celsius to Kelvin: $T = T_C + 273.15$

Kelvin to Celsius: $T_C = T - 273.15$

Note that because temperature measures *average* kinetic energy, it does not depend on the amount of the substance. For example, if you take a spoonful of hot chocolate out of a mug, the temperature of the hot chocolate in the spoon is the same as the temperature of the larger amount of hot chocolate remaining in the mug. The chocolate in the mug, however, has more total thermal energy than the chocolate in the spoon.

What Is Heat?

We are in the unit on heat, and we have described two physical quantities—temperature and thermal energy—but we have not yet discussed heat. So, what exactly is heat? Like *work*, *heat* has a very specific meaning in science. In fact, the concepts of work and heat are closely related. Recall that **work** is energy transferred to an object or system by means of a force acting over a distance. **Heat** is energy transferred to an object or system because of a difference in temperature. Unlike work, however, the transfer of energy as heat occurs at the atomic level. Note that heat, like work, is energy in transition. It is not proper to say that an object or substance "has heat" or "contains heat."

Heat always flows from an object or substance at a higher temperature to an object or substance at a lower temperature. For example, if you put your hand in a cup of hot water, heat will flow from the water to the skin of your hand. The temperature of your skin will increase and the temperature of the water will decrease. If you keep your hand in the water, this exchange of energy will continue until the water and your skin are at the same temperature. When two objects or substances are at the same temperature, they are said to be in *thermal equilibrium*.

Try this experiment sometime: get a cup of hot water (but not scalding), a cup of ice water, and a cup of lukewarm water. Put one hand in the hot water and the other hand in the cold water. Wait a little while, and then move both hands to the lukewarm water. You will find that the hand that was in hot water feels the lukewarm water as cold, while the hand that was in cold water feels the lukewarm water as hot.

This demonstrates that what you sense as hot and cold does not depend directly on the temperature of a substance; the lukewarm water has only one temperature, but you feel it two different ways. What you are actually sensing depends on heat—energy exchanged between the water and your skin to a temperature difference. The temperature of the hand that was in hot water is higher than the temperature of the lukewarm water, so heat flows from your hand to the water. As a result, the water seems cold to you. The temperature of the other hand, the one that was in cold water, is lower than the temperature of the lukewarm water. As a result, heat flows from the water to your hand, and the water seems hot.

Because heat is a form of energy, it has SI units of joules (J). Another common unit of heat is the calorie (cal). A calorie is defined as the amount of energy required to raise the temperature of 1 g of water by 1 degree.

$$1 \text{ cal} = 4.186 \text{ J}$$

A related unit is the Calorie (Cal), with a capital "C." These are the Calories used when talking about the energy in food.

$$1 \text{ Cal} = 1 \text{ kcal} = 4186 \text{ J}$$

Conduction, Convection, and Radiation

There are three primary mechanisms by which energy is transferred as heat: conduction, convection, and radiation. **Conduction** is the transfer of energy as heat between two objects in direct contact. The transfer of energy between your skin and hot water is an example of conduction.

To understand how conduction between the water and your skin takes place, we must zoom in and examine the system at the atomic level. The particles in the water—water molecules—are at a high temperature; they are moving around at fairly high speeds, and therefore have a lot of kinetic energy. The particles in your skin—some water molecules, as well as many different organic molecules—are also moving, but have less kinetic energy on average than the molecules in the hot water. At the point of contact between your skin and the water, the particles in each substance bounce against each other. As this happens, the particles in the hot water transfer some of their kinetic energy to the particles in your skin. Over time, this tends to balance out the average kinetic energy so that the water and your skin have the same temperature. When they are at thermal equilibrium, particles in the two substances are still bumping into each other, and there is still an exchange of energy in both directions, but the net transfer of energy is zero.

Conduction can also happen within an object. For example, if you put a metal spoon in a bowl of hot soup, heat will flow from the soup to the spoon, and then up the handle of the spoon. The conduction within the spoon occurs as particles near the source of the energy—the soup—collide with less energetic particles farther along the spoon.

Not all substances conduct heat equally. Substances that conduct heat well are called *thermal conductors*, while substances that do not conduct heat well are called *thermal insulators*. (These may also be called simply "conductors" and "insulators," but specifying "thermal" distinguishes them from electrical conductors and insulators.) Most metals are good thermal conductors, while most nonmetals are thermal insulators. The difference in thermal conductivity between metal and plastic explains why a metal spoon gets hot fairly quickly in a bowl of hot soup, while a plastic spoon does not.

Convection is the transfer of energy by the movement of fluids with different temperatures. A classic example of convection is a pot of water on a stove. The stove heats the water at the bottom of the pot. As the temperature of this water increases, the water expands slightly, so its density decreases. Because it is now less dense than the water above it, this water rises. But as it does, it cools slightly, and its density decreases again. It then sinks, as more hot water from below rises to take its place. This cycling of a fluid due to temperature and density differences is called a *convection current*.

Note that unlike conduction, in which energy is transferred from one set of particles to another, convection involves the large-scale movement of the particles in the substance. Because particles in a solid are not free to move over large distances, convection occurs only in liquids or gases.

Radiation is the transfer of energy by electromagnetic waves. All objects emit some energy in the form of electromagnetic waves. The total amount of energy emitted in this manner depends on the temperature of the object. When these electromagnetic waves meet another object, some of the waves—particularly those in the infrared part of the electromagnetic spectrum—excite the particles in that object, increasing the kinetic energy of the particles, and therefore increasing temperature.

Electromagnetic waves can travel through a medium, such as air, or they can travel through a vacuum, such as outer space. Most of the energy transferred to Earth from the sun is transferred by radiation.

Specific Heat

When energy is transferred to an object or substance at the atomic level, the heat usually causes an increase in temperature. However, not all substances react to heat in the same way. For example, imagine going to a swimming pool on a hot summer day. The concrete next to the pool might be very hot, as it has been heated by the sun. However, the water in the pool is still cool. That is because a greater amount of energy is required to raise the temperature of water by a given amount than to raise the temperature of concrete by the same amount.

The amount of energy required to raise 1 kg of a substance by 1 degree (1 K or 1°C) is called **specific heat**. Specific heat is also sometimes called *specific heat capacity*. Specific heat is a characteristic physical property of a substance, and different substances have different specific heats. The symbol for specific heat is *c*, and the SI units are J/kg•K or J/kg•°C (because a kelvin is equivalent to a Celsius degree, these units for specific heat are equivalent).

The specific heat of water is 4186 J/kg•K, higher than most substances. The specific heat of concrete varies depending on the type of concrete, but it is generally less than 1000 J/kg•K. Therefore, much less energy is required to raise the temperature of 1 kg of concrete by a certain amount than to raise the temperature of 1 kg of water by the same amount.

The following equation expresses the relationship between heat, specific heat, and temperature change:

heat = specific heat × mass × change in temperature

$$Q = cm\Delta T$$

The quantity *cm* (*specific heat × mass*) is sometimes called *heat capacity*. Therefore, you may sometimes see an equation equivalent to the one above:

heat = heat capacity × change in temperature

Phase Changes

We said above that energy transferred to an object or substance as heat *usually* causes an increase in temperature. However, such energy transfer does not *always* cause an increase in temperature. One case where heat does not cause an increase in temperature is when a phase change is taking place. A phase change is a physical change of a substance from one state of matter (solid, liquid, or gas) to another.

For example, imagine putting a piece of ice at a temperature of −25°C in a saucepan on a hot stove. The stove transfers energy to the pan, which in turn transfers energy to the ice. At first, the energy transferred to the ice causes the temperature of the ice to rise, in accordance with the specific heat equation. However, when the temperature of the ice reaches 0°C, the temperature stops rising, and the ice starts to melt. As the ice is melting, the incoming energy is no longer increasing the kinetic energy of the water molecules in the ice. Instead, the energy is serving to break the bonds that hold the molecules together in a lattice structure. As these bonds are broken, the water changes from a solid to a liquid.

Once all the ice has melted, the temperature of the water will again start to rise as the incoming energy causes an increase in the kinetic energy of the water molecules. This temperature increase will again be in accordance with the specific heat equation. However, when the temperature of the water reaches 100°C, the temperature will again stop rising. The incoming energy now serves to break the weak bonds that hold the water molecules together in the liquid. As this happens, the water starts to vaporize, or turn to a gas (steam).

The energy per unit mass required for a substance to complete a phase change is called **latent heat**. The symbol for latent heat is L, and the SI units are J/kg. The relationship between heat, mass, and latent heat is expressed in the following equation:

$$\textbf{\textit{heat}} = \textbf{\textit{mass}} \times \textbf{\textit{latent heat}}$$

$$Q = mL$$

Latent heat is also involved in phase changes when energy is transferred away from a substance, during freezing (a phase change from liquid to solid) or condensation (a phase change from gas to liquid). The latent heat involved in melting or freezing is called *heat of fusion*, L_f, while the latent heat involved in vaporization or condensation is called *heat of vaporization*, L_v.

Heat Engines

Another case where heat transferred to a system does not strictly increase temperature is when the heat causes the system to do work. A device that converts heat or thermal energy to useful mechanical energy is called a **heat engine**.

Heat engines can be classified many different ways, but one common way to classify them is by the location where the heat is transferred to the system. In an *internal combustion engine*, heat is transferred to the system within the engine itself. The engine of a car is an example of an internal combustion engine. In an internal combustion engine, fuel is compressed in a chamber, then ignited with a spark. The spark causes the fuel to burn, releasing chemical potential energy as heat. This heat causes the fuel and surrounding gases to expand rapidly in an explosion. It is at this point that heat is converted to mechanical energy. The expansion of the fuel drives a *piston*, which in turn

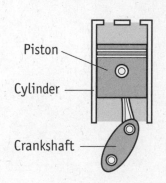

Piston
Cylinder
Crankshaft

drives a *crankshaft*. Ultimately, the work done on the piston and crankshaft is used to turn the wheels of the car. This is a cyclic process. As the crankshaft turns farther, it pushes the piston back into the cylinder. Meanwhile, a new supply of fuel has been added to the cylinder, so the combustion process can occur again.

In an *external combustion engine*, heat is added to the system outside the engine. A steam engine is an example of an external combustion engine. In the operation of a steam engine, water is heated by burning coal or some other fuel. As the water turns to steam, it expands into a cylinder. As it expands further, the steam drives a piston, which in turn drives a flywheel.

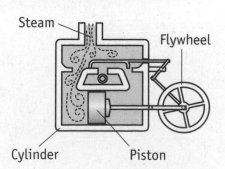

Steam
Flywheel
Cylinder
Piston

Laws of Thermodynamics

The operation of a heat engine, as any machine, is governed by certain physical laws. We have already discussed one such law in the unit on energy: the law of conservation of energy. You may recall that this law says that energy cannot be created or destroyed, although it may change form. In the study of systems involving both work and heat—the science of **thermodynamics**—this law is called the *first law of thermodynamics*. In the case of a heat engine, this law can be interpreted to mean that the work done by the engine cannot be greater than the heat put into the engine.

In the unit on energy, we discussed how in real-world situations, friction always causes some mechanical energy to be converted to thermal energy. This means that the useful work done by a machine is always less than the energy put into the machine.

In other words, no machine is 100% efficient. In thermodynamics, this idea is called the *second law of thermodynamics*. Applied to heat engines, this law can be interpreted to mean that the work done by an engine is always less than the heat put into the engine. This is because some energy always leaks out into the surrounding environment. A more general statement of this law is:

Every transfer of energy involves some loss of useful energy.

You may have heard the term **entropy** used in discussions of energy. Entropy is a measure of the disorder in a system. Wherever there is disorder, there is energy that cannot be harnessed for useful purposes. The second law of thermodynamics can also be expressed in terms of entropy:

Every transfer of energy involves an increase in entropy.

Unit 5, Heat
Physical Science, SV 0425-5

UNIT 5 Review

Darken the circle by the correct answer.

1. What term describes the total kinetic energy of atoms and molecules in a substance?
   - (A) heat
   - (B) temperature
   - (C) thermal energy
   - (D) specific heat

2. What is a measure of the average kinetic energy of atoms and molecules in a substance?
   - (A) heat
   - (B) temperature
   - (C) thermal energy
   - (D) specific heat

3. Which temperature scales have equivalent degree units?
   - (A) Fahrenheit and Celsius
   - (B) Celsius and Kelvin
   - (C) Kelvin and Fahrenheit
   - (D) Fahrenheit, Celsius, and Kelvin

4. What term describes energy transferred due to a difference in temperature?
   - (A) heat
   - (B) work
   - (C) thermal energy
   - (D) specific heat

5. What form of energy transfer involves electromagnetic waves?
   - (A) conduction
   - (B) convection
   - (C) radiation
   - (D) work

6. What form of energy transfer occurs primarily in liquids and gases?
   - (A) conduction
   - (B) convection
   - (C) radiation
   - (D) work

7. What quantity is defined as the amount of energy required to raise the temperature of 1 kg of a substance by 1 degree?
   - (A) heat
   - (B) specific heat
   - (C) latent heat
   - (D) a Calorie

8. What quantity is defined as the energy per unit mass required to complete a change of phase?
   - (A) heat
   - (B) specific heat
   - (C) latent heat
   - (D) a Calorie

Unit 5, Heat
Physical Science, SV 0425-5

Review (cont'd.)

9. Describe what happens when heat is transferred to a substance during a phase change.

_____

_____

_____

10. What does the second law of thermodynamics say about the relationship of work and heat in a heat engine?

_____

_____

_____

UNIT 5    Temperature Conversions

The following equations can be used to convert between the Fahrenheit and Celsius temperature scales:

$$T_C = \frac{5}{9}(T_F - 32.0) \qquad T_F = \frac{9}{5}T_C + 32.0$$

The following equations can be used to convert between the Celsius and Kelvin temperature scales:

$$T = T_C + 273.15 \qquad T_C = T - 273.15$$

Use the temperature conversion equations to complete the table below.

	Fahrenheit	Celsius	Kelvin
Freezing point of water	32.0 °F		
Boiling point of water		100 °C (exact)	
Absolute zero			0 K (exact)
Human body temperature	98.6 °F		
Typical room temperature		22 °C	
Condensation point of helium			4.25 K
Coldest temperature on the moon's surface	−261.4 °F		
Warmest temperature on the moon's surface		117 °C	
Effective temperature at the surface of the sun			5778 K

UNIT 5

Conduction, Convection, and Radiation

There are three primary mechanisms by which energy is transferred as heat: conduction, convection, and radiation.

- **Conduction is the transfer of energy as heat between two objects in direct contact.**

- **Convection is the transfer of energy by the movement of fluids with different temperatures.**

- **Radiation is the transfer of energy by electromagnetic waves.**

For each scenario described below, identify the energy transfer as conduction, convection, or radiation.

1. A thermometer heats up when immersed in a hot liquid. _____

2. Bubbles of gas rise up from the bottom of a pot of boiling water. _____

3. Your face warms up when you are facing toward the sun. _____

4. The flames of a fire rise upward. _____

5. The dark side of the moon is much colder than the side facing the sun. _____

6. Warm, moist air rises upward near the equator. _____

7. The handle of a spoon gets hot when the spoon is in a bowl of hot soup. _____

8. You warm your hands by holding them near a fire. _____

9. Explain why air near the ceiling is usually warmer than air near the floor of a room.

_____

_____

10. Describe, at the atomic level, how energy is transferred to your finger when you place it in a cup of hot water. What type of heat transfer is this?

_____

_____

_____

_____

UNIT 5

Specific Heat

> **Specific heat is the amount of energy required to raise 1 kg of a substance by 1 degree (1 K or 1°C). The following equation shows the relationship between heat, specific heat, mass, and change in temperature:**
>
> **heat = specific heat × mass × change in temperature** $Q = cm\Delta T$

Use the equation to solve the following problems.

1. The element hydrogen has the highest specific heat of all elements. At a temperature of 25°C, hydrogen's specific heat is 1.43×10^4 J/kg•K. If the temperature of a 0.34 kg sample of hydrogen is to be raised by 25 K, how much energy will have to be transferred to the hydrogen as heat? _____

2. The element radon is at the opposite end of the range with the lowest specific heat of all naturally occurring elements. At 25°C, radon's specific heat is 94 J/kg•K. If the temperature of a 0.34 kg sample of radon is to be raised by 25 K, how much energy will have to be transferred to the radon as heat?

_____

3. Lithium has the highest specific heat of any pure metal. The temperature of a 25.00 g sample of lithium will increase by 7.69 K when 684.4 J of energy is added to it. What is lithium's specific heat? _____

4. Brass is an alloy made from copper and zinc. A 0.59 kg brass candlestick has an initial temperature of 98.0°C. If 2.11×10^4 J of energy transfers out of the candlestick as its temperature drops to 6.8°C, what is the specific heat of brass? _____

5. A 0.190 kg piece of copper is heated and fashioned into a bracelet. The amount of energy transferred as heat to the copper is 6.62×10^4 J. If the specific heat of copper is 385 J/kg•K, what is the change in the temperature of the copper? _____

6. Beryllium is used for making rocket parts because of its light weight and sturdiness. It also has a high specific heat that is second only to lithium among pure metals. This specific heat, which is 1825 J/kg•K, gives beryllium a high resistance to temperature change. Suppose a beryllium rocket component with a mass of 1.4 kg is tested at a high temperature and then cooled to 300.0 K. If the heat transferred away from the component is 2.555×10^6 J, what was the component's initial temperature? _____

UNIT 5  Latent Heat and Phase Changes

> The energy per unit mass required for a complete phase change in a substance is called latent heat. The following equation shows the relationship between heat, mass, and latent heat:
>
> $$heat = mass \times latent\ heat \qquad Q = mL$$
>
> Latent heat can be heat of fusion (L_f) for melting and freezing, or heat of vaporization (L_v) for evaporation or condensation.

The graph at right shows the energy required to increase the temperature of 100.0 g of water from below 0°C (when the water is ice) to above 100°C (when the water is steam). Use the graph to answer the following questions.

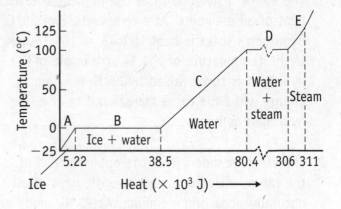

1. During which part(s) of the graph (indicated by letters) is heat causing an increase in temperature? _____

2. During which part(s) of the graph (indicated by letters) is heat causing ice to melt?

   _____

3. During which part(s) of the graph (indicated by letters) is heat causing water to evaporate?

   _____

4. How much heat is required for the full phase change from solid to liquid? (Hint: This is the difference between the two points on the horizontal axis on either side of the phase change.) _____

5. Use your answer from number 4 and the equation for latent heat to find the heat of fusion for water. ($L_f = \dfrac{Q}{m}$)

   _____

6. How much heat is required for the full phase change from liquid to gas?

   _____

7. Use your answer from number 6 and the equation for latent heat to find the heat of vaporization for water.

   _____

UNIT 5

Heat Engines

A heat engine is a device that converts heat or thermal energy to mechanical energy. Heat engines are governed by the first and second laws of thermodynamics.

- **The first law of thermodynamics requires that the work done by an engine cannot be greater than the heat transferred to the engine.**

- **The second law of thermodynamics requires that the work done by an engine is actually less than the heat transferred to the engine.**

Use the diagram to answer the questions.

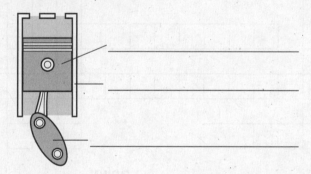

1. What type of heat engine contains the elements pictured above?

   _____

2. Label the following on the diagram above: piston, cylinder, crankshaft.

3. Describe how the engine converts heat to mechanical energy.

   _____

   _____

   _____

   _____

4. If the energy released by one explosion in the chamber is 35 kJ, what does the second law of thermodynamics tell you about the work done on the piston by the expansion in the cylinder?

   _____

   _____

5. If the work done on the crankshaft as a result of the explosion is 12 kJ, what is the efficiency of the engine? $\left(eff = \dfrac{useful\ energy\ output}{energy\ input} \right)$

   _____

   _____

UNIT 5

Heat Crossword

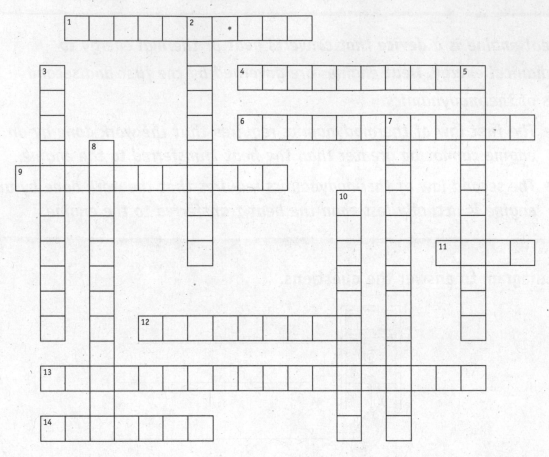

ACROSS

1. Heat transfer by movement within a fluid

4. Energy per unit mass required to complete a phase change

6. Equal to 0 K or −273.15°C

9. A measure of the average kinetic energy of particles

11. Energy transferred due to a temperature difference

12. Energy transferred by electromagnetic waves

13. Occurs when two substances are at equal temperatures

14. A measure of the disorder in a system

DOWN

2. Heat transfer by direct contact

3. A physical change from one state of matter to another

5. A device that measures temperature

7. Total kinetic energy of particles

8. Energy required to increase the temperature of 1 kg of a substance by 1 degree

10. A device that converts heat to mechanical energy

UNIT 6

Waves

We have been discussing energy for the past two units. First we talked about energy in general, and different types of energy and energy transfers at the macroscopic level. We then talked about thermal energy—kinetic energy of particles at the atomic and molecular level—and heat, energy transferred at this level. In this unit, we will talk about a particular, but very common, mechanism for transferring energy: waves.

When you first think of waves, you probably picture waves in the ocean or some other body of water. Waves in water are just one of many examples of waves that you might experience in everyday life. In fact, you are continually surrounded by waves. Sound travels through the air in the form of waves. Light waves carry energy from the sun, and also reflect off of objects and into your eyes, allowing you to see. In today's world, a great deal of information— signals for radio, television, mobile phones, and wireless computer networks—is transmitted through the air as different types of electromagnetic waves.

Key Terms

wave—a disturbance that carries energy through matter or across empty space

medium—the matter through which a wave travels

mechanical wave—a wave that requires a medium in which to travel

transverse wave—a wave in which the motion of particles in the medium is perpendicular to the direction of wave travel

crest—the highest point on a transverse wave

trough—the lowest point on a transverse wave

amplitude—the greatest distance that particles in a medium move away from their normal resting position when a wave passes

wavelength (λ)—the distance between any two successive identical parts of a wave

longitudinal wave—a wave in which the motion of particles in the medium is parallel to the direction of wave travel; also called a compression wave

compression—a region of increased pressure in a longitudinal wave

rarefaction—a region of decreased pressure in a longitudinal wave

electromagnetic wave—a wave caused by a disturbance in electric and magnetic fields; also called a light wave

frequency (f or ν)—the number of waves that pass a point in 1 second

period (T)—the time required for one full wavelength to pass a point

reflection—the turning back of a wave when it meets a surface

refraction—the bending of a wave as it passes from one medium to another

What Are Waves?

A **wave** is a disturbance that carries energy through matter or across empty space. Most waves are *periodic*, which means that they occur in a repeating pattern over time. If you drop a stone into a pond, the stone disturbs the water. The water dips down, bounces back up, and dips down again, several times in a repeating pattern. This disturbance in the water travels outward as a series of circular waves on the surface of the water.

After the waves on the water have settled down, the particles in the water (water molecules) are in pretty much the same place they started. If a fishing bobber were floating in the water, it too would still be in its original location. Waves don't transport matter; they transport energy.

Most types of waves travel through a **medium**. In the case of waves on a pond or in the ocean, the medium is water. Seismic waves—waves created by earthquakes—use Earth itself as the medium. Waves can travel through gases, liquids, or solids. For example, sound waves can travel through air, water, or even a solid wall (although they may be muffled). Waves that require a medium through which to travel are called **mechanical waves**.

Waves are caused by vibrations. When a stone falls into a pond, the water at the surface vibrates up and down. This vibration is similar to the periodic motion of a mass bouncing up and down on a spring. As the water at the point of the stone's entry moves up and down, the water molecules also pull on adjacent molecules, by virtue of the weak bonds that hold the molecules together as a liquid. In this way, the vibration is passed horizontally along the water's surface, and the waves travel outward.

Transverse Waves

In a **transverse wave**, the particles in the medium vibrate up and down, perpendicular to the direction of wave travel. You can create a transverse wave on a rope that is fixed at one end by shaking the free end of the rope up and down. If you keep shaking the rope up and down, you will create a series of waves.

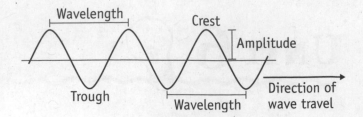

The diagram above shows a series of transverse waves. The high points along the waves are called **crests**, and the low points are called **troughs**. The vertical distance from a crest or trough to the normal resting point of the medium is called the **amplitude**. The distance between two successive crests or troughs is called the **wavelength**. In equations, wavelength is represented by the Greek letter λ (lambda), and uses the same SI units as any length (m, cm, mm, and so on).

Waves on the surface of water are close to being pure transverse waves, but the particles in the wave also have some back-and-forth motion. If you could trace the path of a water molecule—or a fishing bobber or other object floating on the surface—as a wave passed, you would find that the path was circular or elliptical, with both up-and-down motion and back-and-forth motion happening at the same time.

Longitudinal Waves

In a **longitudinal wave**, the particles in the medium vibrate back and forth, parallel to the direction of wave travel. You can create a longitudinal wave in a spring toy that is fixed at one end by shaking the free end of the spring back and forth, in line with the length of the spring. If you keep shaking the spring, you will create a series of waves.

The diagram below shows a longitudinal wave on a spring. As particles move back and forth in a longitudinal wave, they create **compressions**—regions of increased pressure—and **rarefactions**—regions of decreased pressure—in the medium.

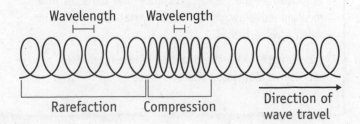

Because they consist of areas of increased and decreased pressure, longitudinal waves are sometimes called *compression waves*. The amplitude of a longitudinal wave is the horizontal distance from a compression or rarefaction to the normal resting point of the medium. (Sometimes the amplitude of a longitudinal wave is measured in units of pressure instead.) The wavelength is the distance between two successive compressions or rarefactions.

Sound waves are an example of longitudinal waves. However, unlike the longitudinal waves on a spring, which move along a straight line, sound waves move in three-dimensional space. Sound waves are produced by a vibrating object, such as the head of a drum or the string on a stringed instrument. The vibration of the object produces compressions and rarefactions in the air (or other medium; sound waves can travel through liquids and solids as well). When sound waves reach your ear, they cause your eardrum to vibrate. These vibrations are converted to electrical nerve signals by cells in your inner ear.

Electromagnetic Waves

The waves we have discussed so far are all mechanical waves that rely on the vibration of particles in a medium. However, there is one class of waves that does not require a medium: **electromagnetic waves**. Electromagnetic waves consist of disturbances in electric and magnetic fields, rather than disturbances in a physical medium. Because electromagnetic waves do not require a physical medium, they are the only waves that can travel through a vacuum, such as outer space.

The diagram below shows the interplay between electric and magnetic fields in an electromagnetic wave. You will learn more about electric and magnetic fields in the next unit. For now, though, you only really need to know one thing: changing electric fields produce magnetic fields, and changing magnetic fields produce electric fields. These two types of fields are always perpendicular to one another in the wave. As electric field strength increases, so does magnetic field strength. As electric field strength decreases, so does magnetic field strength. The wavelength, as with all other waves, is the distance between two successive identical parts of the wave.

Like other kinds of waves, electromagnetic waves can be caused by a vibration. When a charged particle such as an electron vibrates, it can cause fluctuating electric fields that produce electromagnetic waves. Radio waves, for example, are produced by electrons oscillating up and down in an antenna.

Electromagnetic waves span a wide range of wavelengths. The full range of electromagnetic waves make up the *electromagnetic spectrum*. This spectrum includes radio waves, microwaves, infrared light, visible light, ultraviolet light, X rays, and gamma rays. The diagram below shows the wavelengths and frequencies of some of the different regions of the electromagnetic spectrum. As you can see, visible light makes up only a small part of the spectrum.

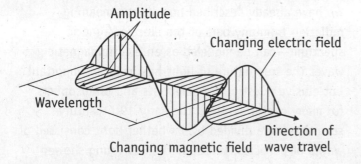

Amplitude
Changing electric field
Wavelength
Changing magnetic field
Direction of wave travel

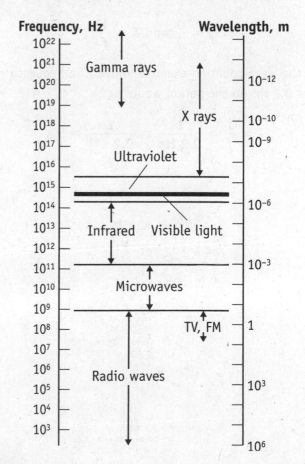

Frequency and Period

Frequency is a measure of the number of waves that pass a point in a given amount of time. The symbol used for frequency in equations is f, or sometimes the Greek letter ν (nu). The SI unit for frequency is hertz (Hz). 1 Hz is equivalent to 1 s^{-1}, or "1 per second."

For example, imagine you are counting the number of waves that pass a fixed point in the water, such as a buoy. If 5 waves pass in a period of 25 seconds, then the frequency of the waves is calculated as follows:

$$f = \frac{5}{25 \text{ s}} = 0.2 \text{ s}^{-1} = 0.2 \text{ Hz}$$

A related quantity is the **period** of the waves. The period is the amount of time for one full wavelength to pass a point. The symbol for the period is T, which you can distinguish from the T for temperature by context.

The period and frequency of a wave are inversely related:

$$frequency = \frac{1}{period} \text{ and } period = \frac{1}{frequency}$$

$$f = \frac{1}{T} \text{ and } T = \frac{1}{f}$$

In the wave-counting example above, the frequency was 0.2 Hz, so the period would be:

$$T = \frac{1}{f} = \frac{1}{0.2 \text{ Hz}} = \frac{1}{0.2 \text{ s}^{-1}} = 5 \text{ s}$$

Frequency is one of the most fundamental and important properties of waves. In sound waves, frequency determines the *pitch* of the sound, or how high or low a sound is. In electromagnetic waves, frequency determines the amount of energy the wave carries. In visible light, frequency also determines color. The frequency of waves is usually determined by the frequency of the vibrations that produce the waves.

Wave Speed

The speed at which waves travel depends on the properties of the medium. For example, sound waves in air at room temperature travel at a speed of about 346 m/s, while sound waves in air at 0°C travel at about 331 m/s. Sound waves in water at room temperature travel much faster, about 1490 m/s. However, for any given medium with constant, uniform properties, wave speed is constant.

No matter what the speed of a wave is, wave speed, frequency, and wavelength always have the same relationship:

$$\textbf{\textit{wave speed = frequency}} \times \textbf{\textit{wavelength}}$$

$$v = f\lambda$$

Note that the equation for wave speed is a simple extension of the general equation for speed:

$$v = \frac{d}{t} = \frac{\lambda}{T} = \frac{1}{T}\lambda = f\lambda$$

The speed of light waves in a vacuum, symbolized by the letter c, is the fastest speed of anything in the universe: $c = 3.00 \times 10^8$ m/s. Light waves do travel more slowly when they are passing through a medium, but in most cases, the difference in speed is very small.

The Nature of Light

We have already described how light—meaning radiation from any part of the electromagnetic spectrum—can be modeled as an electromagnetic wave. The true nature of light has been an important but elusive question for scientists and philosophers for many centuries. Until the early 19th century, scientists were divided over whether light consisted of waves or particles. In 1801, Thomas Young showed that light passed through narrow slits produced interference patterns, which could only be explained if light consisted of waves.

The view that light consists of waves was challenged in the early 20th century, when Albert Einstein showed that when light strikes a piece of metal and dislodges electrons—a phenomenon known as the photoelectric effect—the energy in the light is proportional to the frequency. This is expressed in the following equation:

energy of light = Planck's constant × frequency

$$E = hf$$

This was surprising, because for most waves the energy is proportional to the amplitude, not the frequency. Einstein showed that this could be explained if light consists of packets of energy in discrete amounts. These packets of energy are called *quanta*, and in the case of light are called *photons*. Photons in many respects behave like particles, although they do not have mass.

Since Einstein showed that light consists of photons, most scientists have agreed that neither the wave model nor the particle model alone can explain the true nature of light. Rather, light behaves in some circumstances like a wave and in others like a particle. Which model you choose depends on the situation you are studying.

There is a third model of light, much simpler than the wave model or the particle model, that is useful in studying the behavior of light under certain fairly simple circumstances. This third model depicts light as a *ray*, an imaginary straight line pointing in the direction that the light travels. The ray model is not meant to show the true nature of light; it is simply a useful device for representing light on diagrams.

Reflection

When light passes from one medium to another, it may behave in a number of different ways. If the new medium is transparent, some or all of the light might pass through it. If the new medium is not transparent, then some of the light will be absorbed and some will be reflected. **Reflection** is the turning back of a wave when it meets a surface.

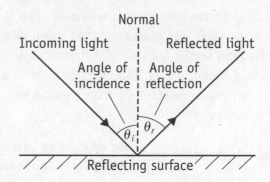

When light hits a rough surface, it is reflected in many different directions. This is known as *diffuse reflection*. Diffuse reflection is very common; most of the objects that you see in the world are reflecting light diffusely, and it is this reflected light that reaches your eyes. The color of an object is determined by the color (or combination of colors) of light that it reflects. All other colors of light are absorbed by the object.

When light hits a very smooth surface, such as a mirror, the light may be reflected in a single direction. Light in this case follows the *law of reflection*, which states:

The angle of incidence equals the angle of reflection.

$$\theta_i = \theta_r$$

The *angle of incidence* is the direction of the incoming light, and the *angle of reflection* is the angle of the reflected light. Both of these angles are measured from the *normal*, an imaginary line perpendicular to the surface at the point of incidence. Note that if the surface is curved, then the normal line is perpendicular to the line tangent to the surface. The diagram above illustrates the angle of reflection.

Refraction

When light passes from one transparent medium to another, the path of the light may bend. The bending of a wave as it passes from one medium to another is called **refraction**.

You can see a simple example of refraction if you place a straight object, such as a pencil, partway into a glass of water. The part of the object that is in the water appears displaced from the rest of the object because light from the object is refracted when it passes from water into glass (and then again into air).

Refraction occurs because of different wave speeds in different media. The speed of light in a medium can be represented by a ratio called the *index of refraction, n*:

$$\textit{index of refraction} = \frac{\textit{speed of light in vacuum}}{\textit{speed of light in medium}}$$

$$n = \frac{c_v}{c_m}$$

The index of refraction of a vacuum is exactly 1, while the index of refraction for any other medium is greater than 1. Because it is a ratio, the index of refraction has no units.

When light passes from a medium with a lower index of refraction to a medium with a higher index of refraction, such as from air to glass, the light slows down and bends toward the normal, as shown in the diagram below.

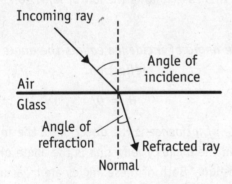

Conversely, when light passes from a medium with a higher index of refraction to a medium with a lower index of refraction, such as from glass to air, the light speeds up and bends away from the normal, as shown in the diagram below.

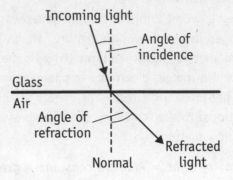

The relationship between the indices of refraction and the angles of the rays is given by an equation known as *Snell's law*:

$$n_i \sin\theta_i = n_r \sin\theta_r$$

If you know any three of the variables in this equation, you can find the fourth one. Finding one of the angles can be a bit tricky, however, as it involves an inverse sine. For example, to find θ_r:

$$\theta_r = \sin^{-1}\left(\frac{n_1}{n_2}\sin\theta_i\right)$$

Lenses, such as those found in eyeglasses, use refraction to bend light to a focal point. *Prisms* can use refraction to separate white light into a rainbow of colors. This is possible because different colors (frequencies) of light move at different speeds in a medium. Higher frequency light, such as blue and violet light, bends more than lower frequency light, such as red and orange. The separation of light into component colors is called *dispersion*.

UNIT 6

Review

Darken the circle by the correct answer.

1. In what kind of wave do particles move up and down perpendicular to the direction of wave travel?

   Ⓐ transverse wave

   Ⓑ longitudinal wave

   Ⓒ electromagnetic wave

   Ⓓ sound wave

2. What kind of wave can travel through empty space?

   Ⓐ transverse wave

   Ⓑ longitudinal wave

   Ⓒ electromagnetic wave

   Ⓓ sound wave

3. In what direction do particles move in a sound wave?

   Ⓐ They move perpendicular to the direction of wave travel.

   Ⓑ They move parallel to the direction of wave travel.

   Ⓒ They move both perpendicular and parallel to the direction of wave travel.

   Ⓓ The particles do not move in a sound wave.

4. What term describes the maximum displacement of a particle in a wave?

   Ⓐ a crest

   Ⓑ a trough

   Ⓒ wavelength

   Ⓓ amplitude

5. Which of the following could be used to measure wavelength in a longitudinal wave?

   Ⓐ the distance between two adjacent compressions

   Ⓑ the distance between two adjacent rarefactions

   Ⓒ the distance between two successive crests

   Ⓓ both A and B

6. What is the relationship between the period and the frequency of a wave?

   Ⓐ They are directly proportional.

   Ⓑ They are the inverse of one another.

   Ⓒ The period is the frequency divided by time.

   Ⓓ They are equal.

7. Which of the following is determined by the frequency of waves?

   Ⓐ the pitch of sound

   Ⓑ the energy of light

   Ⓒ the color of light

   Ⓓ all of the above

8. State the law of reflection.

   _____

   _____

UNIT 6

Transverse and Longitudinal Waves

Answer the questions about waves.

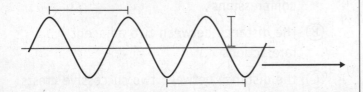

1. What kind of wave is pictured above?

   _____

2. Label the following on the wave above: crest, trough, wavelength, amplitude, direction of travel.

3. In what direction would the particles in this wave move, relative to the direction of wave travel?

   _____

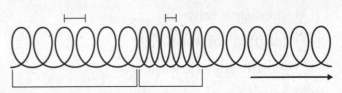

4. What kind of wave is pictured above?

   _____

5. Label the following on the wave above: compression, rarefaction, wavelength, direction of travel.

6. In what direction would the particles in this wave move, relative to the direction of wave travel?

   _____

For each wave described below, identify the wave as more like a transverse wave or a longitudinal wave.

7. The wave created by moving the end of a spring toy up and down

   _____

8. The wave created by moving the end of a spring toy back and forth parallel to the length of the spring

   _____

9. A sound wave

   _____

10. An ocean wave

    _____

11. An electromagnetic wave

    _____

UNIT 6  Frequency, Period, Wavelength, and Wave Speed

> *Frequency measures the number of waves that pass a point every second, while period measures the number of seconds it takes for a full wavelength to pass. Frequency and period have an inverse relationship:*
>
> $$\text{frequency} = \frac{1}{\text{period}} \qquad f = \frac{1}{T} \qquad\qquad \text{period} = \frac{1}{\text{frequency}} \qquad T = \frac{1}{f}$$
>
> *Wave speed is the product of frequency and wavelength:*
>
> $$\text{wave speed} = \text{frequency} \times \text{wavelength} \qquad v = f\lambda$$

Use the equations above to solve the following problems.

1. Waves in a lake are 6 m apart and pass a person on a raft every 2 s. What is the frequency, period, wavelength, and speed of the waves?

_____

2. A buoy bobs up and down in the ocean. The waves have a wavelength of 2.5 m, and they pass the buoy at a speed of 4.0 m/s. What is the frequency of the waves? How much time does it take for one wave to pass under the buoy?

_____

3. A sound wave with a frequency of 60.0 Hz travels through steel with a wavelength of 85.5 m. What is the speed of this wave?

4. Yellow light with a wavelength of 589 nm travels through quartz glass with a speed of 1.94×10^8 m/s. What is the frequency of the light?

_____

5. Earthquakes generate shock waves that travel through Earth's interior. The fastest of these waves are longitudinal waves called *primary waves*, or *p-waves*. A p-wave has a very low frequency, typically around 0.050 Hz. If the speed of a p-wave with this frequency is 8.0 km/s, what is its wavelength?

_____

6. Earthquakes also produce transverse waves that move more slowly than the p-waves. These waves are called *secondary waves*, or *s-waves*. If the wavelength of an s-wave is 2.3×10^4 m, and its speed is 4.5 km/s, what is its frequency?

_____

UNIT 6 — The Electromagnetic Spectrum

The following table shows the range of wavelengths or the range of frequencies for the major parts of the electromagnetic spectrum. Complete the table by filling in the missing ranges. Use the equation $c = f\lambda$, where $c = 3.00 \times 10^8$ m/s. Then mark and label each of these regions between the wavelength and frequency scales at the bottom of the page. Note that the X ray and gamma ray regions overlap.

Region	Wavelength range	Frequency range
radio waves	> 30 cm	< 1.0×10^9 Hz
microwaves	30 cm — 1 mm	1.0×10^9 Hz — 3.0×10^{11} Hz
infrared (IR) waves	1 mm — 700 nm	
visible light	700 nm (red) — 400 nm (violet)	
ultraviolet (UV) light		7.5×10^{14} Hz — 5.0×10^{15} Hz
X rays		5.0×10^{15} Hz — 3.0×10^{21} Hz
gamma rays	0.1 nm — 10^{-5} nm	

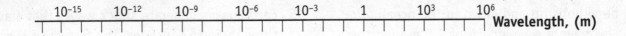

10^{-15} 10^{-12} 10^{-9} 10^{-6} 10^{-3} 1 10^3 10^6 **Wavelength, (m)**

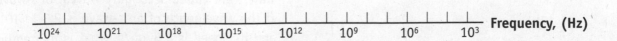

10^{24} 10^{21} 10^{18} 10^{15} 10^{12} 10^9 10^6 10^3 **Frequency, (Hz)**

UNIT 6 — The Law of Reflection

> When light hits a very smooth surface, such as a mirror, the light follows the law of reflection, which states that the angle of incidence equals the angle of reflection:
>
> $$\theta_i = \theta_r$$
>
> The angle of incidence is the direction of the incoming light, and the angle of reflection is the angle of the reflected light. Both of these angles are measured from the normal, an imaginary line perpendicular to the surface.

The diagrams below show an incoming light ray striking a surface. On each diagram, draw the normal line, then draw the reflected ray. Label the angle of incidence and the angle of reflection on each diagram.

1.
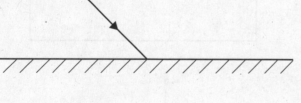

2.

3.

4.
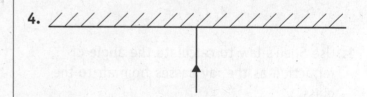

The diagram at right shows 5 incoming light rays striking a curved surface. The surface has the shape of a parabola. At each point of incidence, draw a normal line (perpendicular to the tangent). Then draw the reflected rays.

5.
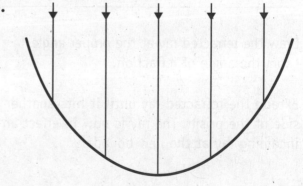

Unit 6, Waves
Physical Science, SV 0425-5

UNIT 6  Refraction and Snell's Law

> When light passes from one transparent medium to another, the light may bend, or refract. The path of the light can be calculated using Snell's law:
>
> $$n_i \sin\theta_i = n_r \sin\theta_r$$
>
> In this equation, n_i is the index of refraction for the medium of the incoming light ray, and θ_i is the angle of incidence; n_r is the index of refraction for the medium of the refracted light ray, and θ_r is the angle of refraction.

The diagram at right shows an incoming ray of light, in air, meeting the surface of a glass rectangular prism. The angle of incidence is 30.0°. The index of refraction for air is 1.00, and the index of refraction for the glass is 1.52. Use the diagram to answer the questions.

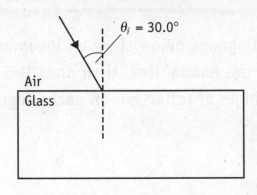

1. Use Snell's law to calculate the angle of refraction as the ray passes from air to the glass.

_____

2. Draw the refracted ray at the proper angle. Label the angle of refraction.

3. Extend the refracted ray until it hits another side of the prism. The ray is now in effect an incoming ray at the new boundary.

4. Use Snell's law to calculate the angle of refraction as the ray passes from the glass back into the air.

_____

5. Draw a normal line at the new point of incidence, then draw the refracted ray at the proper angle. Label the angle of incidence and the angle of refraction.

6. How does the direction of the ray coming out of the prism compare to the original ray before it went into the prism?

_____

Unit 6, Waves
Physical Science, SV 0425-5

UNIT 6

Waves Word Find

Find the answers to the following in the word find puzzle below.

```
C R I M X C V H J L Y D O Y R U
G W V Y A R X Z W H A G O I M I
J A N C B L S L G Z J K R P P D
C V U Z R G C Y A L P O U E F H
O E Y B H E Z R K K W C B X N I
M L N B H Q S K W S R Z E M P E
P E H M E G B T Z D V E U N I F
R N B E H M U N D Y H I K E M G
E G F G J L L O Z I D D D Y I D
S T M S M H V K R E J H C T I P
S H X Z E Z W O M T C N Y O T K
I R A R E F A C T I O N V Q M M
O F T N O J L B R R O L F L A K
N Z A W X A Q Q C O F L C X O E
N O I T C A R F E R K O A A D U
R B V W T P Q Q W N T R X C R G
```

1. What waves carry through matter or space

   _____

2. The matter through which a wave travels

   _____

3. The highest point on a transverse wave

   _____

4. The lowest point on a transverse wave

   _____

5. A region of increased pressure in a longitudinal wave

   _____

6. A region of decreased pressure in a longitudinal wave

   _____

7. The distance between any two successive identical parts of a wave

   _____

8. The units for frequency

   _____

9. An imaginary line pointing in the direction that light travels

   _____

10. The bending of a wave as it passes from one medium to another

    _____

Unit 6, Waves
Physical Science, SV 0425-5

UNIT 7  Electricity and Magnetism

Electricity and magnetism are ever present in our daily lives. Many of the conveniences of modern life depend on electric power, whether supplied by a battery or a wall socket. Computers and other electronic devices use complex electrical circuits to perform complex tasks. You probably have magnets holding pictures or notes to your refrigerator at home.

Electricity and magnetism are both derived from a single, fundamental kind of force: electromagnetic force.

Electromagnetic forces play many important roles at the foundation of the physical world. We have already discussed how electromagnetic waves—ranging from radio waves to visible light to X rays—are propagated by fluctuating electric and magnetic fields. Many forces that appear to involve direct contact, such as friction, or even something as simple as a bat hitting a baseball, are the result of electromagnetic forces at the microscopic level. All electric and magnetic phenomena come, ultimately,

Key Terms

electric charge (q)—a fundamental property of matter that causes electric force

electric force (F_e)—the attractive or repulsive force between two charged objects due to electric charge

electric field—the region around a charged object in which another charged object experiences a force because of its charge

electrical potential energy (PE_{elec})—the potential energy associated with a charged object due to its position in an electric field

electric potential (V)—electrical potential energy per unit charge

potential difference (ΔV)—the difference in electric potential between two points in an electric field; also called *voltage*

voltage (ΔV)—potential difference

current (I)—the rate at which positive charge flows through a conductor

resistance (R)—a measure of the degree to which a conductor resists the movement of electrons; the ratio of ΔV to I in a conductor

electric circuit—a set of electrical components joined together so they provide one or more complete paths for a current

series—describes electrical components connected so that they provide only one pathway for current

parallel—describes electrical components connected so that they provide more than one pathway for current

magnetic pole—one of two areas in a magnet where magnetic force seems to be strongest

magnetic force (F_B)—the attractive or repulsive force between two magnetized objects or on a charge moving in a magnetic field

magnetic field—a region in which magnetic force can be detected

domain—a microscopic region in which the magnetic fields of atoms are aligned

from the most fundamental particles that make up the material world—the protons and electrons that make up atoms.

Electric Charge

If you rub a balloon against your hair, you will find that the balloon attracts your hair, pulling strands away from your head. If you rub a second balloon against your hair, you will find that the two balloons will repel one another. These attractive and repulsive forces are due to **electric charge**. Electric charge is a fundamental property of matter. Just as mass is a fundamental property that causes gravitational force, electric charge is a fundamental property that causes electric force.

Gravitational force is always attractive, but electric force can be either attractive or repulsive. That is because there are two different kinds of charge. In the 18th century, Benjamin Franklin, one of the founding fathers of the United States, first suggested the terms *positive* and *negative* to describe these two kinds of charge. When two objects with like charge (positive and positive or negative and negative) are near each other, the charges cause a repellant force. When objects with opposite charge (positive and negative) are near each other, the charges cause an attractive force.

In the balloon example, rubbing the balloon against your hair gives your hair a net positive charge and the balloon a net negative charge. As a result, your hair and the balloon have opposite charges, and attract, while the two balloons have like charges, and repel.

We now know that a net positive or negative charge on an object is due to an imbalance in the number of protons and electrons in the object. Recall that most forms of matter are composed of *atoms*. Atoms are the smallest units of an element, such hydrogen, oxygen, iron, and so on. *Molecules*, which are the smallest units of compounds such as water, ammonia, sugar, and so on, are made of two or more atoms. All atoms are composed of three fundamental kinds of particles: *protons* and *neutrons*, which are concentrated in the nucleus of an atom, and *electrons*, which reside in energy levels surrounding the nucleus. Protons have a positive charge, electrons have a negative charge, and neutrons have no charge.

In a neutral atom or molecule, the number of electrons equals the number of protons, so the negative and positive charges balance out. However, if the number of electrons does not equal the number of protons, the atom or molecule will have a net charge. An atom or molecule with a net (nonzero) charge is called an *ion*.

Usually, ions form by adding or removing electrons. That is because electrons are more loosely bound in an atom than protons. Protons are held in the nucleus by very strong nuclear forces; the number of protons in an atom only changes as a result of a nuclear reaction. In the balloon example, the friction between your hair and the balloon causes electrons to move from your hair to the balloon. This creates some positive ions in your hair and some negative ions in the balloon. As a result, your hair has a net positive charge while the balloon has a net negative charge.

The SI units of electric charge are coulombs (C), and the symbol for charge is q. The charge of an electron is the smallest possible charge:

$$q_e = -1.6 \times 10^{-19} \text{ C}$$

The charge on a proton has the same magnitude as the charge on an electron, but is positive:

$$q_p = +1.6 \times 10^{-19} \text{ C}$$

The net charge on an ion is always some multiple of the charge on an electron or proton. For example, an aluminum ion, Al^{+3}, has three more protons than electrons, so its net charge is

$$3q_p = 3 \times (1.6 \times 10^{-19} \text{ C}) = 4.8 \times 10^{-19} \text{ C}$$

Electric Force

The **electric force** between two charged particles or objects depends on the two charges and on the distance between them. This is expressed mathematically by Coulomb's law:

$$\text{electric force} = C \times \frac{\text{charge 1} \times \text{charge 2}}{\text{radius}^2}$$

$$F_e = C \frac{q_1 q_2}{r^2}$$

The C in this equation is a constant called the *Coulomb constant*, or sometimes the *electrostatic constant*.

$$C = 8.99 \times 10^9 \text{ N} \bullet \text{m}^2/\text{C}^2$$

Compare Coulomb's law on the previous page to Newton's law of universal gravitation:

$$\textit{force of gravity} = G \times \frac{\textit{mass 1} \times \textit{mass 2}}{\textit{radius}^2}$$

$$F_g = G\frac{m_1 m_2}{r^2}$$

Electric force, like any other force, is a vector quantity and has units of newtons (N). If you are considering the force between only two objects, a positive value means the force is repulsive, while a negative value means the force is attractive.

Electric Fields

A useful concept for modeling electric forces is the concept of an **electric field**. An electric field is defined as the region around a charged object in which another charged object experiences a force because of its charge.

The strength of an electric field at any given point is defined by the force that would act on a charge at that point divided by that charge:

$$\textit{electric field strength} = \frac{\textit{electric force on a charge}}{\textit{charge}}$$

$$E = \frac{F_e}{q}$$

Electric field strength has units of N/C.

It follows that you can find the force on a charge at a point if you know the electric field strength at that point:

force on a charge = charge × electric field strength

$$F_e = qE$$

On diagrams, electric fields can be represented by *electric field lines*. The following diagrams show the electric field lines around a) a particle with a +1 charge and b) a particle with a −2 charge. The arrows indicate

the direction of the force that a positively charged particle would experience in the field. That is why the lines around the positive charge point away from the charge, while the lines around the negative charge point toward the charge. The density of the lines—that is, the number of lines in a given area on the diagram—is proportional to the strength of the field. For example, there are more lines around the −2 charge than around the +1 charge. Note also that in each diagram, the line density decreases as you move away from the particle. This reflects the fact that the electric force is inversely proportional to the distance from the charge.

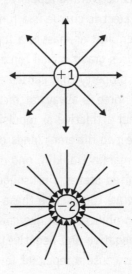

It is often useful to depict 3-dimensional electric fields on a 2-dimensional diagram. The diagram on the left below shows how field lines pointing "out of the page" are represented. The symbol of a circle with a dot in the middle is meant to suggest the head of an arrow as it would appear if it were coming straight out of the page toward you. The diagram on the right shows how field lines pointing "into the page" are represented. The circle with an "X" in the middle is meant to suggest the tail of an arrow as it would look going away from you down into the page. Each of the fields in the diagrams is a *uniform field*, meaning the strength of the field is the same at every point.

Uniform electric field
Out of the page

Uniform electric field
Into the page

Electrical Potential Energy and Voltage

When you lift an object above Earth's surface, you do work on the object, giving it energy. If the object is held at rest above Earth's surface, the energy is in the form of gravitational potential energy. You may recall that the equation for this energy is as follows:

$$PE_g = mgh$$

This energy is equal to the work done on the object: the force ($F_g = mg$) times the distance (h). Similarly, if you move a charged object in an electric field, you do work against an electric force, and the object gains **electrical potential energy**. This is equal to the force ($F_e = qE$) times the distance (d) away from a reference point in the field:

electrical PE = −charge × field strength × distance

$$PE_{elec} = -qEd$$

The negative sign is in the equation because the potential energy of a positive charge will decrease as its distance from the source of the field increases. The distance, d, is defined with respect to some arbitrary point in the field that you have picked to be the zero point.

Electric potential is a quantity closely related to electrical potential energy. Electric potential is the electrical potential energy *per unit charge*. Mathematically, this is calculated as follows:

$$V = \frac{PE_{elec}}{q}$$

Because electric potential is measured with reference to an arbitrary point, it is more common (and generally more useful) to measure the *difference* in electric potential between two points in an electric field. This quantity is called **potential difference**.

$$potential\ difference = \frac{change\ in\ electrical\ PE}{charge}$$

$$\Delta V = \frac{\Delta PE_{elec}}{q}$$

If we combine this equation with the equation for electrical potential energy, we can find the equation for potential difference in a uniform electric field:

$$\Delta V = \frac{\Delta PE_{elec}}{q} = \frac{\Delta(-qEd)}{q} = -E\Delta d$$

potential difference = −field strength × distance between points

Another term for potential difference is **voltage**. The SI unit for potential difference is volts (V). The voltage of a typical AA battery is 1.5 V. That means that if a charge of 1.0 C moved from one terminal of the battery to the other, the change in the electrical potential energy on the charge would be 1.5 J.

Current

When charged particles are in an electric field, they experience forces that cause them to move from a position of higher potential energy to a position of lower potential energy. Moving electric charge is called **current**. More specifically, current is defined as the amount of charge that passes a point in a given amount of time:

$$current = \frac{charge}{time}$$

$$I = \frac{q}{t}$$

The SI unit for current is amperes (A), and the symbol for current is I.

By convention, current is considered the movement of positive charges. However, most electric currents are actually due to the movement of electrons, which are negatively charged. For example, if you make a closed circuit by attaching wires to the two terminals of a battery, as shown on the next page, electrons will flow from the negative terminal to the positive terminal. The current, however, will be considered to flow from the positive terminal to the negative terminal. This works out alright, because in terms of electric charge and electric fields, the movement of negative charges in one direction is equivalent to the movement of positive charges in the opposite direction.

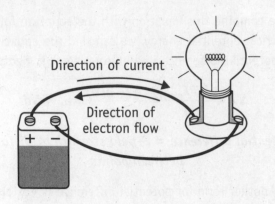

Direction of current

Direction of
electron flow

Current that always flows in the same direction is called *direct current* (DC). The current created by a battery is direct current. A typical electrical socket in your home provides *alternating current* (AC). Alternating current switches direction back and forth very rapidly, usually changing direction about 60 times per second.

Materials in which electrons can flow easily are called *electrical conductors*. Most metals are good electrical conductors. Materials in which electrons do not flow easily are called *electrical insulators*. Plastic and glass are both examples of electrical insulators. A typical electric cord consists of two conducting metal wires (usually copper), surrounded by an insulating plastic sheath. The plastic blocks the flow of electrons, so you can safely touch the cord even when current is flowing through the wires.

Resistance and Ohm's Law

When a potential difference exists between two points in a conductor, current will flow. However, the amount of current that flows for a given potential difference depends on the **resistance** of the conductor. Resistance is a measure of the degree to which a conductor resists the movement of electrons. Quantitatively, resistance is defined as the ratio of potential difference to current:

$$resistance = \frac{potential\ difference}{current}$$

$$R = \frac{\Delta V}{I}$$

The SI unit for resistance is ohms, represented symbolically by the Greek letter Ω (omega). Ohms are equivalent to volts per ampere.

The definition of resistance makes a lot of sense if you think about it. If a conductor has a high potential

difference, but the current is small, then the conductor must be offering a lot of resistance to the current. On the other hand, if a relatively large current results from a relatively low potential difference, the conductor must be offering little resistance. Good conductors have low resistance, while poor conductors (insulators) have high resistance. Certain materials, called *superconductors*, have zero resistance when they are cooled below a certain critical temperature. Sometimes, electric circuits include devices whose only purpose is to increase resistance. These devices are called *resistors*.

For many materials used in electrical devices, including most metals, the resistance is constant over a wide range of potential differences. These materials follow Ohm's law, which is expressed by the following equation:

$$\frac{\Delta V}{I} = constant$$

Materials and electrical devices for which this is true are said to be *ohmic*. When you are working with systems that obey Ohm's law, you can calculate current or voltage using these rearranged forms of the definition of resistance:

$$\Delta V = IR \qquad I = \frac{\Delta V}{R}$$

Unless a problem specifically states otherwise, you can assume the materials in the problem are approximately ohmic, so you can rearrange the resistance equation to solve for either ΔV or I.

Electric Circuits

An **electric circuit** is a set of electrical components joined together so they provide one or more complete paths for a current. Circuits can contain many different types of components. Some common components found in circuits are wires, switches, resistors, light bulbs, and sources of potential difference, such as batteries or AC outlets. If the pathway for current is continuous, the circuit is called a *closed circuit*. If the pathway is broken, such as by a switch or a disconnected wire, the pathway is called an *open circuit*.

Unit 7, Electricity and Magnetism
Physical Science, SV 0425-5

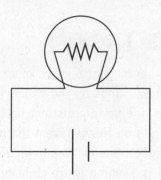

Circuits are represented on *schematic diagrams*. The schematic diagram above represents the simple circuit with a battery and a light bulb discussed earlier. The two short parallel lines represent a battery; the longer of the two lines is the positive terminal, and the shorter line is the negative terminal. The other straight lines on the diagram are wires. The zig-zagging line in a circle represents a light bulb.

Series and Parallel Circuits

When components in a circuit are connected in **series**, they form a single pathway for current. Components connected in **parallel** provide more than one pathway for current. For example, the diagram below shows a string of decorative lights arranged a) in series and b) in parallel. The two small parallel lines in a circle on the left side of each circuit represent the plug to an AC outlet.

a)

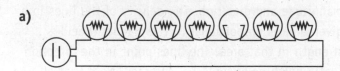

b)

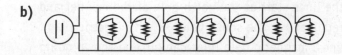

Note that one bulb in each circuit is missing a filament. In the series circuit, that means the pathway for the current is broken, so no current can flow through the circuit. As a result, every light in the string will be dark even when the plug is plugged in.

In the parallel circuit, on the other hand, each bulb is on a separate pathway for current. As a result, one bulb going out will not open the circuit for the other bulbs. Only the bulb with the missing filament will be dark; the others will light up.

Electric Power

Almost every electrical device that you use requires a continuous supply of power, such as a battery or an AC outlet. A power source provides the potential difference that drives current in the device. In the units on energy and heat, we saw that power is defined as the rate at which energy is transferred. In the case of electrical devices, electric power is the rate at which a device converts electrical energy to other forms of energy.

Because all circuits have some resistance, some of the energy put into a circuit is used to overcome the resistance. This always results in some energy being dissipated as heat. Some of this dissipation of energy may be desirable. For example, electric heaters, toaster ovens, and electric ranges use the energy dissipated in a high-resistance wire or coil to provide heat. In a light bulb, some of the energy dissipated by resistance in the filament is released as light.

The primary equation for calculating electric power is as follows:

electric power = current × potential difference

$$P = I\Delta V$$

For devices that follow Ohm's law, you can also use any of the following equations to calculate electric power:

$$P = I^2 V$$

$$P = \frac{(\Delta V)^2}{P}$$

As with other forms of power, the SI unit for electric power is watts (W). Recall that a watt is equivalent to transferring 1 J of energy every second. So, a 100 W light bulb converts 100 J of electrical energy to light and heat every second.

Most power companies that provide electrical energy to your home report energy usage in units of kilowatt-hours (kW•h). Note that these are units of energy, not power. A kilowatt is a unit of power, that is, energy divided by time; multiplying a kilowatt by a unit of time (hours) results in units of energy. The following conversion shows the relationship between watts and kilowatt-hours:

$$1 \text{ kW}\bullet\text{h} \times \frac{10^3 \text{ W}}{\text{kW}} \times \frac{60 \text{ min}}{\text{h}} \times \frac{60 \text{ s}}{\text{min}} = 3.6 \times 10^6 \text{ W}\bullet\text{s}$$

$$= 3.6 \times 10^6 \frac{\text{J}}{\text{s}} \bullet\text{s} = 3.6 \times 10^6 \text{ J}$$

So, 1 kW•h is equivalent to 3.6×10^6 J.

Magnets and Magnetic Force

You have probably, at some time in your life, played with magnets, seeing how they interact with other magnets. If you have, you probably realized that magnets, like electric charges, sometimes attract one another and sometimes repel one another.

Every magnet has two **magnetic poles**: a north pole and a south pole. North poles of magnets are so called because they tend to point toward north if they are free to rotate, as in a compass. South poles, on the other hand, point south. You have learned that with electric charges, like charges repel one another while opposite charges attract. In magnets, like poles repel while opposite poles attract. So, if you hold the north pole of one magnet near the north pole of another magnet, you will feel a **magnetic force** pushing the poles away from each other.

Objects that maintain their magnetic properties over time are called *permanent magnets*. Magnets are also able to temporarily magnetize other objects, making them *temporary magnets*. For example, if you hold a permanent magnet near a paper clip, the magnet causes the paper clip to become magnetized temporarily. An attractive magnetic force then pulls the paper clip toward the magnet.

Magnetic Fields

If you place a bar magnet under a piece of paper, then sprinkle iron filings on the paper, you will see the iron filings line up in a distinct pattern around the magnet. The iron filings reveal the **magnetic field** around the magnet. Similar to an electric field, a magnetic field is a region in which magnetic force can be detected. Magnetic fields can be detected with an easily magnetized object, such as the iron filings, or with a permanent magnet, such as in a compass.

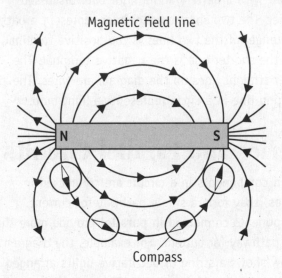

Magnetic field line

N   S

Compass

The diagram above shows a cross-section of the magnetic field around a bar magnet. As with electric field lines, the lines in a magnetic field reflect both magnitude and direction. The density of the lines in a given area is proportional to the magnetic field strength in that area. The lines point in the direction that a north pole would be attracted. Note that all the lines start at the north pole of the magnet and terminate at the south pole. As with electric field lines, magnetic field lines can also be shown going "into the page" or "out of the page."

Magnetic field strength has SI units of teslas (T). The symbol for magnetic field strength is B.

Magnetism from Electric Current

You have learned that electric fields are created by electric charges. Magnetic fields, it turns out, are created by *moving* electric charges.

For example, if you put several sensitive compasses near a straight wire carrying a current, you will find that the compass needles all line up along concentric circular paths perpendicular to the wire. The magnetic field around a straight, current-carrying wire follows a "right-hand rule." If you imagine wrapping your right hand around the wire with your thumb pointing in the direction of the current, your curved fingers will point in the direction of the magnetic field, as shown in the diagram below.

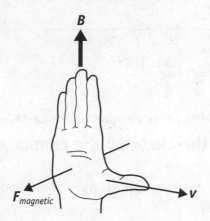

Current

Magnetic Field

So what about the magnetic fields around a magnet? Are they also caused by moving electric charges? Yes, they are. As electrons spin around inside atoms, they create tiny magnetic fields. In most atoms, the magnetic fields of the electrons in the atom tend to cancel each other out. However, in certain materials, mostly metals, the magnetic fields caused by spinning electrons do not cancel out. Furthermore, the magnetic fields tend to affect nearby electrons, so that whole regions of matter can have magnetic fields all aligned in one direction. Such a region is called a **domain**. A magnet—whether permanent or temporary—contains many such domains all lined up with the magnetic fields pointing the same direction. These combine to produce the overall magnetic field around the magnet.

Charges Moving in Magnetic Fields

When an electric charge moves in a magnetic field, the charge experiences a magnetic force. The direction of this force is both perpendicular to the velocity of the charged particle and to the magnetic field. You can find this direction with another "right-hand rule," as shown in the diagram that follows. With this right-hand rule, imagine lining up your fingers with the

field and your thumb with the velocity, or with the component of the velocity that is perpendicular to the field. The magnetic force is then directed away from your palm.

The magnitude of the magnetic force on a moving charge is given by the following equation:

magnetic force = charge × velocity × magnetic field strength

$$F_B = qvB$$

This relationship also serves to define the magnetic field strength quantitatively:

$$B = \frac{F_B}{qv}$$

The force only applies to the component of velocity that is perpendicular to the magnetic field. If the velocity is not entirely perpendicular to the field, you can find the magnetic field strength with the equation:

$$F_B = qvB\sin\theta$$

where θ is the angle between the velocity and the field.

Because the magnetic force is perpendicular to the velocity of a charged particle, the force acts as a centripetal force, causing the path of the particle to curve. If the magnetic field is uniform, the charged particle will move in a circular path in the field.

UNIT 7   Review

Darken the circle by the correct answer.

1. What causes an ion to have a net negative charge?

   Ⓐ It has more protons than electrons.

   Ⓑ It has more electrons than protons.

   Ⓒ It has fewer protons than neutrons.

   Ⓓ It has fewer neutrons than electrons.

2. Which of the following do electric force and gravitational force NOT share in common?

   Ⓐ They both depend on the inverse square of distance.

   Ⓑ They both depend on fundamental properties of matter.

   Ⓒ They both act by means of a field.

   Ⓓ They can both be either attractive or repulsive.

3. Which of the following is equivalent to the term *voltage*?

   Ⓐ electrical potential energy

   Ⓑ electric potential

   Ⓒ potential difference

   Ⓓ electric field strength

4. What is a measure of the amount of charge passing a point in a given time interval?

   Ⓐ voltage

   Ⓑ current

   Ⓒ resistance

   Ⓓ electric power

5. How is the direction of current defined by convention?

   Ⓐ Current is in the same direction that the charges move.

   Ⓑ Current is in the direction opposite the direction that the charges move.

   Ⓒ Current is in the direction that positive charge moves.

   Ⓓ Current is in the direction that negative charge moves.

6. What kind of material has zero resistance when cooled below a critical temperature?

   Ⓐ a conductor

   Ⓑ an insulator

   Ⓒ a semiconductor

   Ⓓ a superconductor

7. What is true in electrical devices that obey Ohm's law?

   Ⓐ Potential difference is constant.

   Ⓑ Current is constant.

   Ⓒ Resistance is constant.

   Ⓓ Temperature is constant.

8. What happens when the north poles of two magnets are brought close together?

   _____

   _____

UNIT 7 Electric Charge and Electric Force

The electric force between two charged particles or objects can be calculated with Coulomb's law:

$$\text{electric force} = C \times \frac{\text{charge 1} \times \text{charge 2}}{\text{radius}^2} \qquad F_e = C \frac{q_1 q_2}{r^2}$$

$$C = 8.99 \times 10^9 \ N\bullet m^2/C^2$$

The electric force on a charge can also be calculated if you know the electric field strength at the charge's location:

$$\text{force on a charge} = \text{charge} \times \text{electric field strength} \qquad F_e = qE$$

The charge of a proton is 1.6×10^{-19} C and the charge on an electron is -1.6×10^{-19} C. The mass of a proton is 1.67×10^{-27} kg and the mass of an electron is 9.11×10^{-31} kg.

Use the information to answer the questions.

1. A calcium ion, Ca^{+2}, has 20 protons.

   a) How many electrons does the ion have? _____

   b) What is the net charge of the ion? _____

2. Two balloons each have a net charge of 4.0×10^{-7} C.

   a) How many electrons must have been removed from each balloon to give them this charge? _____

   b) What is the force of one balloon on another if the balloons are 15 cm apart? _____

   c) Is the force attractive or repulsive?

   _____

3. A hydrogen atom consists of one proton and one electron. The average distance between the proton and the electron is about 5.3×10^{-11} m.

   a) Find the magnitude of the electric force between these two particles. _____

   b) Use Newton's law of universal gravitation $(F_g = G\frac{m_1 m_2}{r^2}$, where $G = 6.67 \times 10^{-11}$ $N\bullet m^2/kg^2$) to find the magnitude of the gravitational force between these two particles. _____

   c) How does the gravitational force compare to the electric force in the atom?

   _____

   _____

UNIT 7  Potential Difference, Current, and Resistance

Resistance is defined quantitatively with the following equation:

$$\text{resistance} = \frac{\text{potential difference}}{\text{current}} \qquad R = \frac{\Delta V}{I}$$

Use the definition of resistance to solve the following problems. You can also assume that Ohm's law holds true in each problem, so that you may rearrange the equation to solve for ΔV or I. Remember that voltage is another term for potential difference.

1. A television set is plugged into a 120-V outlet. The current in the television is equal to 0.75 A. What is the overall resistance of the television set? _____

2. A clothes dryer is equipped with an electric heater. The heater works by passing air across an electric wire that is hot because of the current in it. The wire's resistance is 10.0 Ω, and the current in the wire equals 24 A. What is the voltage across the heater wire? _____

3. You have probably heard that high voltages are more dangerous than low voltages. To understand this, assume that your body has a resistance of 1.0×10^5 Ω. What voltages would have to be across your body to produce the following currents?

   a) 5.0 mA, which would cause a tingling feeling _____

   b) 10.0 mA, which would be a fatal amount of current _____

   c) 1.0 A _____

4. A window-unit air conditioner has an overall resistance of 22 Ω. If the voltage across the air conditioner equals 115 V, what is the current in the air conditioner's circuit? _____

5. While in another country, you should always find out the voltage that is used in that country before you plug in an appliance. To understand the reason for this precaution, do the following calculations for a laptop computer that is designed to draw 3.0 A at 115 V.

   a) Calculate the resistance of the computer.

   _____

   b) Calculate the current that the same computer would draw if you plugged it into a 220-V outlet, which is common in countries other than the United States.

   _____

UNIT 7   Series and Parallel Circuits

The diagrams below show two different circuits that could be used for a string of five decorative lights. Each light acts as a resistor, and the resistance of each light is 8.0 Ω.

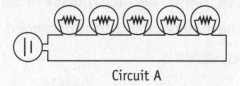

Circuit A _____

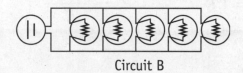

Circuit B _____

Use the diagrams to answer the questions.

1. To the right of each circuit, label the circuit as either a series circuit or a parallel circuit.

2. For resistors in a series circuit, the total resistance across all resistors equals the sum of each individual resistor: $R_{tot} = R_1 + R_2 \ldots$ What is the total resistance in the series circuit above? _____

3. Use the equation $I = \dfrac{\Delta V}{R}$ to calculate the total current in the series circuit if $\Delta V = 115$ V. Each bulb in the circuit will have this amount of current through it. _____

4. For resistors in a parallel circuit, the total resistance in the circuit is found using the sum of reciprocals: $\dfrac{1}{R_{tot}} = \dfrac{1}{R_1} + \dfrac{1}{R_2} + \ldots$ What is the total resistance in the parallel circuit above? _____

5. Use the equation $I = \dfrac{\Delta V}{R}$ to calculate the total current in the parallel circuit if $\Delta V = 115$ V.

_____

6. Each bulb in the parallel circuit will have $\dfrac{1}{5}$ of the total current. What is the current through one bulb in the parallel circuit? _____

7. A bulb with more current through it will be brighter than a bulb with less current. Which circuit has the brightest lights? _____

8. Describe what would happen if the filament broke in the middle bulb of Circuit A.

_____

_____

9. Describe what would happen if the filament broke in the middle bulb of Circuit B.

_____

_____

_____

UNIT 7   Electric Power

Electric power is the rate at which electrical energy is converted to other forms of energy. This can also be considered as the power dissipated in an electric circuit or electrical device. The following equations, and rearranged versions of them, can be used to calculate electric power:

$$P = I\Delta V \qquad\qquad P = I^2 R \qquad\qquad P = \frac{(\Delta V)^2}{R}$$

Use the information to answer the questions.

1. A generator produces electricity with a voltage of 2.5×10^4 V and a current of 20.0 A. How much power does the generator produce?

_____

2. An alarm clock uses 5.0 W of electric power. If the clock is plugged into a 120-V outlet, what electric current is in the clock's circuit?

_____

3. A nightlight uses 4.00 W of power when plugged into an outlet. Assume that the only resistance in the circuit is provided by the light bulb's filament. The current in the circuit is 3.40×10^{-2} A. What is the voltage across the filament? _____

4. Fuel cells are chemical cells that combine hydrogen and oxygen gas to produce electrical energy. In recent years, a fuel cell has been developed that can generate 1.06×10^4 W of power. If the cell produces a current of 16.3 A, what is the voltage across the cell? _____

5. Several appliances in a house contribute to the home's overall energy consumption. Calculate the power use of each of the following appliances if they are each plugged into 120.0-V outlets:

a) a toaster ($R = 18.0\ \Omega$) _____

b) an air conditioner ($R = 24.0\ \Omega$) _____

c) an electric lamp ($R = 192\ \Omega$) _____

d) Calculate the total power use of these three appliances. _____

6. A computer with a resistance of 57.5 Ω has a power input of 230.0 W. Using the equations that relate power to resistance, calculate:

a) the voltage across the computer. _____

b) the current in the computer. _____

UNIT 7

The Magnetic Field Around a Wire

> When current passes through a straight wire, the current creates a magnetic field in concentric circles around the wire. The direction of the field is determined by a "right-hand rule" as shown in the diagram at right.

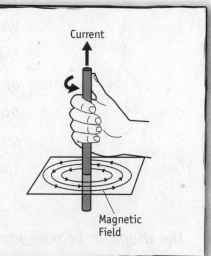

Current

Magnetic Field

For diagrams 1 and 2, draw and label an arrow showing the direction of the current in the wire.

For diagrams 3 and 4, draw symbols showing the direction of the magnetic field above and below the wire.

1.

⊙ ⊙ ⎮⎮ ⊗ ⊗
⊙ ⊙ ⎮⎮ ⊗ ⊗
⊙ ⊙ ⎮⎮ ⊗ ⊗
⊙ ⊙ ⎮⎮ ⊗ ⊗

3.

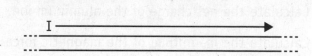

I ⟶

2.

⊗ ⊗ ⎮⎮ ⊙ ⊙
⊗ ⊗ ⎮⎮ ⊙ ⊙
⊗ ⊗ ⎮⎮ ⊙ ⊙
⊗ ⊗ ⎮⎮ ⊙ ⊙

4.

⟵ I

Unit 7, Electricity and Magnetism
Physical Science, SV 0425-5

UNIT 7

Charges Moving in Magnetic Fields

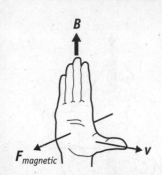

When a charged particle is moving in a magnetic field, the particle experiences a magnetic force. The direction of the force is perpendicular to the field and to the particle's velocity, according to the right-hand rule as shown at right. The magnitude of the force is given by the equation:

$$F_B = qvB$$

The diagram below shows the path of an aluminum ion, Al^{+3}, in a uniform magnetic field directed into the page. The velocity of the ion is 2.0×10^4 m/s, and the strength of the magnetic field is 7.5×10^{-3} T. Remember that the charge of a proton is 1.6×10^{-19} C.

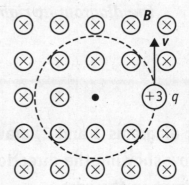

Use the information and diagram to answer the questions.

1. Calculate the net charge of the aluminum ion. _____

2. Calculate the magnitude of the magnetic force on the ion. _____

3. Draw an arrow on the diagram showing the direction of the magnetic force on the ion.

4. The strength of the magnetic field is changed so that the force on the ion is 1.5×10^{-14} N. What is the new magnitude of the magnetic field?

_____

_____

5. Describe how the path of the ion would be different if the magnetic field were pointed out of the page instead of into the page.

_____

_____

_____

UNIT 7

Electricity and Magnetism Crossword

ACROSS

4. A circuit that provides more than one path for current

5. An atom or molecule with a net charge

7. SI units for electric power

8. SI units for current

9. Region of matter in which magnetic fields are aligned

11. SI units for electric charge

12. SI units for resistance

13. A negatively charged subatomic particle

14. A material in which charge does not flow easily

DOWN

1. Every magnet has two of these

2. A region in which a charged object experiences electric force

3. Current that rapidly changes direction

6. The SI units for magnetic field strength

10. Another term for potential difference

GLOSSARY

acceleration (*a*)—a vector quantity that measures the change in velocity over a given time interval (p. 22)

accuracy—how close a measured quantity is to its actual value (p. 6)

amplitude—the greatest distance that particles in a medium move away from their normal resting position when a wave passes (p. 88)

buoyant force (*F_B*)—the upward force that a fluid exerts on a submerged or floating object (p. 39)

centripetal acceleration (*a_c*)—acceleration directed toward the center of a circular path (p. 24)

centripetal force (*F_c*)—any force that causes centripetal acceleration, or acceleration that results in a curved path of motion (p. 38)

chemical potential energy—energy stored in the chemical bonds that bind atoms to one another (p. 56)

compound machine—a device composed of two or more simple machines (p. 58)

compression—a region of increased pressure in a longitudinal wave (p. 88)

conduction—the transfer of energy as heat between two objects in direct contact (p. 75)

convection—the transfer of energy by the movement of fluids with different temperatures (p. 76)

conversion factor—a ratio between two different units of measurement that is equal to 1 (p. 4)

crest—the highest point on a transverse wave (p. 88)

current (*I*)—the rate at which positive charge flows through a conductor (p. 103)

density (*D*)—a measurement of mass per unit volume (p. 38)

domain—a microscopic region in which the magnetic fields of atoms are aligned (p. 107)

efficiency—the ratio of useful work output to work input in a machine (p. 59)

elastic potential energy—energy stored in a stretched or compressed medium (p. 55)

electric charge (*q*)—a fundamental property of matter that causes electric force (p. 101)

electric circuit—a set of electrical components joined together so they provide one or more complete paths for a current (p. 104)

electric field—the region around a charged object in which another charged object experiences a force because of its charge (p. 102)

electric force (*F_e*)—the attractive or repulsive force between two charged objects due to electric charge (p. 101)

electric potential (*V*)—electrical potential energy per unit charge (p. 103)

electrical energy—energy associated with charged particles (p. 56)

electrical potential energy (*PE_elec*)—the potential energy associated with a charged object due to its position in an electric field (p. 103)

electromagnetic wave—a wave caused by a disturbance in electric and magnetic fields; also called a light wave (p. 89)

energy—the ability to move or change matter (p. 54)

entropy—a measure of the disorder in a system (p. 78)

force (*F*)—the cause of an object's acceleration; a vector quantity equal to the product of the object's mass and its acceleration (p. 33)

frequency (*f* or *ν*)—the number of waves that pass a point in 1 second (p. 90)

friction (*F_f*)—a force that opposes the motion between two surfaces that are in contact (p. 39)

GLOSSARY

gravitational potential energy (PE_g)—potential energy due to an object's position in a gravitational field (p. 55)

heat (Q)—energy transferred at the atomic level due to a temperature difference (p. 75)

heat engine—a device that converts heat or thermal energy to useful mechanical energy (p. 77)

impulse—a vector quantity equal to force multiplied by a time interval (p. 35)

inertia—the tendency for an object to remain at rest or to continue moving at a constant velocity unless acted upon by an unbalanced force (p. 33)

kinetic energy (KE)—energy associated with an object due to the object's motion (p. 55, 73)

kinetic friction (F_k)—the friction between two contacting surfaces that are moving relative to one another (p. 40)

latent heat (L)—the energy per unit mass required for a substance to complete a phase change (p. 77)

longitudinal wave—a wave in which the motion of particles in the medium is parallel to the direction of wave travel; also called a compression wave (p. 88)

magnetic field—a region in which magnetic force can be detected (p. 106)

magnetic force (F_B)—the attractive or repulsive force between two magnetized objects or on a charge moving in a magnetic field (p. 106)

magnetic pole—one of two areas in a magnet where magnetic force seems to be strongest (p. 106)

mass (m)—a measure of the amount of matter in an object (p. 34)

mechanical advantage (MA)—the ratio of the output force to the input force in a machine (p. 58)

mechanical wave—a wave that requires a medium in which to travel (p. 88)

medium—the matter through which a wave travels (p. 88)

momentum (p)—a vector quantity equal to the product of an object's mass and its velocity (p. 34)

normal force (F_n)—a reaction force perpendicular to the surface of contact between two objects (p. 36)

nuclear energy—energy that binds protons and neutrons together inside the nucleus of an atom (p. 56)

parallel—describes electrical components connected so that they provide more than one pathway for current (p. 105)

period (T)—the time required for one full wavelength to pass a point (p. 90)

potential difference (ΔV)—the difference in electric potential between two points in an electric field; also called *voltage* (p. 103)

potential energy (PE)—energy that is stored within a system (p. 55)

power (P)—the rate at which energy is transferred (p. 57)

precision—the exactness of a measurement (p. 6)

projectile motion—the motion of an object influenced only by gravity (p. 23)

radiation—the transfer of energy by electromagnetic waves (p. 76)

rarefaction—a region of decreased pressure in a longitudinal wave (p. 88)

reflection—the turning back of a wave when it meets a surface (p. 91)

refraction—the bending of a wave as it passes from one medium to another (p. 91)

resistance (R)—a measure of the degree to which a conductor resists the movement of electrons; the ratio of ΔV to I in a conductor (p. 104)

GLOSSARY

scientific notation—a method of notation in which numbers have one nonzero digit to the left of the decimal point, the remaining digits to the right of the decimal point, and are multiplied by a power of ten (p. 5)

series—describes electrical components connected so that they provide only one pathway for current (p. 105)

significant figures—the digits in a physical quantity that are known with certainty, plus one uncertain digit (p. 6)

simple machine—a simple device that redistributes force when doing work (p. 57)

specific heat (c)—the amount of energy required to raise the temperature of 1 kg of a substance by 1 degree (1 K or 1°C) (p. 76)

speed (v)—a measurement of the distance an object moves in a given time interval (p. 21)

static friction (F_s)—the friction between two contacting surfaces that are at rest relative to one another (p. 39)

temperature (T)—a measure of the average kinetic energy of particles within an object or substance (p. 74)

thermal energy (U)—the total kinetic energy of particles within an object or substance (p. 56, 74)

thermodynamics—the scientific study of the relationship between heat and other forms of energy (p. 78)

transverse wave—a wave in which the motion of particles in the medium is perpendicular to the direction of wave travel (p. 88)

trough—the lowest point on a transverse wave (p. 88)

vector—a quantity that has both magnitude and direction (p. 8)

velocity (v)—a vector quantity that measures both speed and direction of motion (p. 22)

voltage (ΔV)—potential difference (p. 103)

wave—a disturbance that carries energy through matter or across empty space (p. 88)

wavelength (λ)—the distance between any two successive identical parts of a wave (p. 88)

weight (F_g)—the force of gravity on an object (p. 36)

work (W)—energy transferred by a force; a quantity equal to the product of the force on an object and the distance the object moves (p. 55, 75)

Answer Key

Unit 1 — Tools of Physical Science

Review, pp. 10–11

1. D	2. C	3. D	4. B
5. A	6. D	7. B	8. D

9. $v = \sqrt{\dfrac{2KE}{m}}$ 10. 39.4 in.

Units of Measurement, p. 12

1. B	2. C	3. G	4. A
5. I	6. H	7. J	8. D
9. F	10. E		

Converting Units, p. 13

1. 0.745		2. 0.1	
3. 351		4. 4.5×10^{-6}	
5. 2.5×10^{-5}		6. 1.2×10^{9}	
7. 5×10^{-3}		8. 1.2×10^{-2}	
9. 38	10. 24	11. 59	12. 556
13. 4.61	14. 3.78	15. 91.5	16. 0.79
17. 47	18. 21	19. 56	20. 16

Scientific Notation, p. 14

1. 1.2×10^{3} 2. 1.2×10^{-3}
3. 5.7×10^{1} 4. 3.5×10^{6}
5. 6×10^{0} 6. 1,470 m/s
7. 0.00000001 cm   8. 384,000 km
9. 5.49×10^{-4} amu
10. 1.66×10^{8} km²; 4.2×10^{3} m
11. 5×10^{-3} cm/h; 2×10^{-2} cm/h
12. 2×10^{4} Hz; 1.5×10^{5} Hz

Significant Figures, p. 15

1. 1	2. 2	3. 2	4. 1
5. 3	6. 2	7. 6	8. 2

9. 28.5 cm²
10. 574 kg•m/s²
11. 1.7×10^{2} m³ or 170 m³
12. 60 km/h
13. 2.70 kg
14. 17.5 m
15. 15.00 m or 1.50×10^{3} cm
16. 1.3 L or 1.3×10^{3} mL

Taking Measurements, pp. 16–17

1. 14.85 cm
2. 1 h, 16 min, 33.74 s
3. 48.5 mi/h
4. 14.1 °C
5. 11.2 mV
6. 1.40 V
7. digital stopwatch (2), digital voltmeter (5)
8. ruler (1), speedometer (3), thermometer (4), analog voltmeter (6)

Working with Equations, p. 18

1. $\dfrac{F_g}{g}$ 2. $-\dfrac{F}{k}$

3. $\dfrac{V}{I}$; $\dfrac{V}{R}$ 4. vt; $\dfrac{d}{v}$

5. $v_i + at$; $v_f - at$ 6. $\dfrac{5}{9}(T_F - 32)$

7. $\dfrac{v^2}{a_c}$; $\sqrt{a_c r}$ 8. $\dfrac{2KE}{v^2}$; $\sqrt{\dfrac{2KE}{m}}$

9. $\dfrac{F_g r^2}{Gm_1}$; $\sqrt{G\dfrac{m_1 m_2}{F_g}}$ 10. $\dfrac{v^2}{2g}$; $\sqrt{2gh}$

Vectors, p. 19

1. The resultant vector should go up and to the right, connecting the open base of one vector to the open head of the other, completing a triangle.
2. The resultant vector should go up and to the left, connecting the open base of one vector to the open head of the other, completing a triangle.
3. The resultant vector should go down and to the right, connecting the open base of one vector to the open head of another, completing a quadrilateral.
4. 7.8 m/s
5. 4.5 m/s

ANSWER KEY cont'd.

Tools of Physical Science Crossword, p. 20

ACROSS
1. accuracy
3. meniscus
5. precision
9. scientific notation
10. meters
11. parallax

DOWN
2. conversion factor
4. kilograms
6. nanosecond
7. vector
8. newtons

Unit 2 — Motion

Motion Review, p. 25

1. A
2. B
3. B
4. C
5. C
6. D
7. C
8. An object can accelerate without changing speed if the direction of the velocity changes. Examples may vary. One example is a ball whirled on a string in circular motion.

Speed and Velocity, p. 26

1. 90 km/h
2. 25 m/s to the west or 90 km/h to the west
3. −25 m/s or −90 km/h
4. 7.5×10^3 m = 7.5 km
5. 9.4×10^4 m = 94 km
6. 3.0×10^5 m = 3.0×10^2 km
7. 2.0×10^3 m = 2.0 km
8. 27 s

Graphing Speed, p. 27

1. The line should match the data, starting at the origin and increasing up and to the right, with a slight, gradual increase in slope.
2. The slope gradually increases with time.
3. 13.3
4. m/s

5.

Time (s)	Total distance (m)	Average speed (m/s)
1.0	4.0	4
2.0	10	6
3.0	18	8
4.0	27	9
5.0	37	10
6.0	48	11
7.0	59	11
8.0	71	12
9.0	83	12
10.0	96	13
10.3	100	13.3

6. Average speed is the same as the slope on the graph.

Acceleration, p. 28

Problem	Equation used	Variable solving for	Solution
1.	$a = \dfrac{(v_f - v_i)}{t}$	a	5.0 m/s²
2.	$d = v_i t + \dfrac{1}{2} at^2$	d	9.2 m
3.	$d = \dfrac{1}{2}(v_i - v_f)t$	t	6.0 s
4.	$v_f^2 = v_i^2 + 2gd$	v_f	9.5 m/s
5.	$v_f^2 = v_i^2 + 2gd$	d	1.3 m

Speed and Acceleration Graphs, p. 29

1. d
2. b
3. c
4. e
5. a

ANSWER KEY cont'd.

Projectile Motion, p. 30

1. no
2. yes
3. 7.5 m/s
4. 13 m/s
5. 7.5 m/s
6. −6.6 m/s
7. 10 m/s
8. −41°
9. Yes; because the angle is negative, the ball is moving downward, so it must already have reached its peak height.
10. 1.3 s
11. 8.6 m

Centripetal Acceleration, p. 31

1. Centripetal acceleration should be an arrow pointing toward the center of the circle. Tangential velocity should be an arrow tangent to the circle pointing straight ahead of the car. The radius of curvature should be the radius of the circle.
2. Centripetal acceleration is perpendicular to tangential velocity.
3. The centripetal acceleration would increase by 4 times.
4. 7.2 m/s^2
5. 64 m
6. 11 m/s

Motion Word Find, p. 32

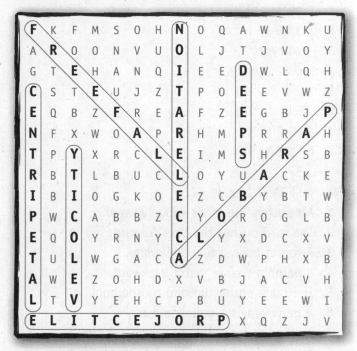

1. speed
2. velocity
3. acceleration
4. free fall
5. projectile
6. parabola
7. centripetal

Unit 3 — Force

Force Review, pp. 41–42

1. C
2. B
3. B
4. A
5. C
6. D
7. A
8. C
9. D
10. Static friction is friction between two surfaces that are at rest relative to one another. Kinetic friction is friction between two surfaces in relative motion.

Answer Key
Physical Science, SV 0425-5

ANSWER KEY cont'd.

Newton's Second Law, p. 43

1. 2.28×10^3 N
2. -1.86×10^7 N
3. -448 m/s^2
4. -6.12 m/s^2
5. 1.2×10^7 kg
6. 9.5×10^4 kg
7. **a.** 0.2 N
   b. 1.8 kg

Newton's Third Law, p. 44

1. Air pushes the bird's wings upward.
2. The road pushes the tires forward.
3. A rocket pushes fuel downward.
4. A dolphin pushes water backward.
5. The table pushes upward on the book.
6. A gun propels a bullet forward.
7. A reaction force cannot cancel out the corresponding action force because the two forces always act on two different objects.

Momentum and Impulse, p. 45

1. 5.6×10^{10} kg•m/s
2. 1.6×10^{10} kg•m/s
3. 4.0×10^{10} kg•m/s
4. 8.5×10^5 m/s
5. 40.2 m/s
6. -11.7 kg•m/s
7. -46.8 N

Force Diagrams, p. 46

1. F_g and F_n should still be the same as in the initial diagram. F_e should be of greater magnitude than F_f.
2. F_g and F_n should still be the same as in the initial diagram. F_f should be of greater magnitude than F_e.
3. The only forces on the car should be F_g and F_n, and these should still be the same as in the initial diagram.

4. The car is angled upward as if climbing a hill. $F_{g,x}$ should point forward parallel to the road. F_f should point backward parallel to the road, and should equal $F_{g,x}$ in magnitude. $F_{g,y}$ should point downward, perpendicular to the road. F_n should point upward, perpendicular to the road, and should equal $F_{g,y}$ in magnitude.

Mass and Weight, pp. 47–48

1. 1.40×10^3 N
2. 143 kg
3. 143 kg
4. 233 N
5. 52.4 lb
6. Answers will vary, but students should use the following equations:
   weight in N = weight in lb $\times$ 4.45 N/lb;
   mass in kg = weight in N/9.81 m/s^2.
7. Answers will vary, but students should use the following equations:
   weight in N = mass in kg $\times$ 1.63 m/s^2;
   weight in lb = weight in N $\times$ 1 lb/4.45 N.
8. An astronaut in orbit has weight because Earth is exerting a gravitational force on the astronaut. The astronaut experiences apparent weightlessness because the spacecraft is falling with the same rate of acceleration as the astronaut.

Forces in Orbital Motion, p. 49

1. 1.98×10^{20} N
2. 1.98×10^{20} N
3. toward Earth
4. 1.02×10^3 m/s
5. 3.52×10^{22} N
6. 3.52×10^{22} N
7. 2.97×10^4 m/s

ANSWER KEY cont'd.

Density, p. 50

1. 1 kg
2. The ball will sink.
3. The oil will float on top of the water.
4. 0.534 g/cm^3
5. 6.0×10^4 kg
6. 4.29×10^3 cm^3
7. 3.16×10^{-15} g/cm^3
8. 1×10^{15} g

Buoyancy, p. 51

1. 4.4×10^{-2} kg
2. 0.43 N
3. 3.4×10^{-2} m^3
4. 34 kg
5. 3.3×10^2 N
6. 3.3×10^2 N
7. 0 N
8. 0.43 N

Friction, p. 52

1. 4.4 N
2. 4.4 N
3. 2.7 N
4. 2.7 N
5. 2.2 N
6. 4.9 m/s^2
7. 3.8 N
8. 2.4 N
9. 2.2 N
10. 1.9 N
11. The book will not start sliding on its own because the maximum static friction is greater than the component of the weight that is parallel to the tabletop.

Force Crossword, p. 53

ACROSS

2. weight
4. gravity
9. coefficient of friction
10. inertia
11. force

DOWN

1. newtons
3. friction
5. density
6. momentum
7. reaction force
8. buoyant force

Unit 4 — Energy

Energy Review, pp. 60–61

1. D
2. A
3. C
4. B
5. B
6. D
7. C
8. C
9. B
10. lever, pulley, wheel and axle, inclined plane, wedge, screw; Examples will vary.

Kinetic Energy, p. 62

1. 2.3×10^4 J
2. 2.0×10^{-2} J
3. 0.15 kg
4. 1.04×10^6 kg
5. 78 m/s
6. 1.5×10^2 m/s
7. 28.9 m/s

Gravitational Potential Energy, p. 63

1. 3.2×10^5 J
2. 6.5×10^3 J
3. 2.7 J
4. 15 m/s
5. 81.9 kg
6. 9.6×10^2 kg
7. 2.45 m
8. 1.50×10^6 m

Work, p. 64

1. 2.3×10^4 J
2. 2.38×10^5 J
3. 2.38×10^5 J
4. 27 N
5. 38.0 m
6. 2.7 J
7. 3.9 J

Conservation of Energy in a Simple Pendulum, pp. 65–66

1. 0.86 J
2. 0 J
3. Gravitational potential energy is transformed into kinetic energy.
4. 0 J
5. 0.86 J
6. 2.6 m/s
7. Kinetic energy is transformed into gravitational potential energy.
8. 0.35 m
9. The total energy of the system is conserved/constant.
10. No; total energy is still conserved. Some of the mechanical energy has been transformed into other forms of energy (such as thermal energy).

ANSWER KEY cont'd.

Power, p. 67

1. 5.0×10^3 W
2. 1.2×10^7 W
3. 5×10^8 W
4. 9.80×10^7 J
5. 4.1×10^2 J
6. 9.30 s
7. 9.6×10^2 s

Simple Machines, pp. 68–69

1. lever
2. wheel and axle
3. pulley
4. inclined plane
5. screw
6. wedge
7. Diagrams should be similar to those in the background information.
8. Answers may vary. Possible answers include a seesaw and a prying bar.
9. Diagrams should be similar to those in the background information.
10. Answers may vary. Possible answers include a wheelbarrow and a door.
11. Diagrams should be similar to those in the background information.
12. Answers may vary. Possible answers include a broom and a pair of tweezers.
13. Wheel and axle (e.g., the wheels, the pedals), screw (e.g., screw attaching the handlebars to the frame), lever (e.g., the brake levers).

Mechanical Advantage, p. 70

1. 8.00
2. 3.3
3. 1.8×10^3 N
4. 261 N
5. 46.8 N
6. 1.28×10^3
7. The input distance of an inclined plane is always greater than the output distance, so the mechanical advantage must be greater than 1.

Efficiency, p. 71

1. 0.37 or 37%
2. 0.24 or 24%
3. 505 J
4. 290 kJ
5. 776 J
6. 2.8×10^5 J
7. There must be no friction in the machine, so that mechanical energy is conserved.

Energy Word Find, p. 72

1. joule
2. mechanical
3. work
4. power
5. watt
6. fulcrum
7. compound machine
8. efficiency

Unit 5 — Heat

Heat Review, pp. 79–80

1. C
2. B
3. B
4. A
5. C
6. B
7. B
8. C
9. The energy does not cause a change in temperature. Instead, the energy serves to break the bonds holding particles in the substance together.
10. The work done by a heat engine is always less than the heat transferred to the engine.

ANSWER KEY cont'd.

Temperature Conversions, p. 81

Fahrenheit	Celsius	Kelvin
32.0 °F	**0.00 °C**	**273.15 K**
212 °F	100 °C (exact)	**373.15 K**
460 °F	**−273.15 °C**	0 K (exact)
98.6 °F	**37.0 °C**	**310 K**
72 °F	22 °C	**295 K**
−452 °F	**−269 °C**	4.25 K
−261.4 °F	**−163.0 °C**	**110 K**
243 °F	117 °C	**390 K**
9941 °F	**5505 °C**	5778 K

Conduction, Convection, and Radiation, p. 82

1. conduction
2. convection
3. radiation
4. convection
5. radiation
6. convection
7. conduction
8. radiation
9. Warm air is less dense than cool air, so it tends to rise above cool air.
10. Water molecules in the hot water collide with atoms and molecules in your finger, transferring kinetic energy to the particles in your finger. This tends to increase the average kinetic energy (temperature) in your finger and decrease the average kinetic energy (temperature) in the water. This is an example of conduction.

Specific Heat, p. 83

1. 1.2×10^5 J
2. 8.0×10^2 J
3. 3.56×10^3 J/kg•K
4. 3.9×10^2 J/kg•°C
5. 905 K
6. 1.3×10^3 K

Latent Heat and Phase Changes, p. 84

1. A, C, E
2. B
3. D
4. 3.33×10^4 J
5. $L_f = 3.33 \times 10^5$ J/kg
6. 2.26×10^5 J
7. $L_v = 2.26 \times 10^6$ J/kg

Heat Engines, p. 85

1. internal combustion engine
2. The students' labels should match the labels shown in the diagram in the background information.
3. Fuel in the cylinder is ignited with a spark, causing the fuel to burn. This converts chemical potential energy in the fuel to heat. The heat causes the fuel and surrounding gases to expand rapidly. The expansion of the fuel and gases does work on the piston, which in turn does work on the crankshaft.
4. It must be less than 35 kJ.
5. 0.34, or 34%

Heat Crossword, p. 86

ACROSS
1. convection
4. latent heat
6. absolute zero
9. temperature
11. heat
12. radiation
13. thermal equilibrium
14. entropy

DOWN
2. conduction
3. phase change
5. thermometer
7. thermal energy
8. specific heat
10. heat engine

Unit 6 — Waves

Waves Review, p. 93

1. A   **2.** C   **3.** B   **4.** D

5. D   **6.** B   **7.** D

8. The angle of incidence equals the angle of reflection.

Transverse and Longitudinal Waves, p. 94

1. a transverse wave

2. Labels should match those in the diagram of a transverse wave in the Background Information.

3. perpendicular to the direction of wave travel

4. a longitudinal wave

5. Labels should match those in the diagram of a longitudinal wave in the Background Information.

6. parallel to the direction of wave travel

7. transverse wave

8. longitudinal wave

9. longitudinal wave

10. transverse wave

11. transverse wave

Frequency, Period, Wavelength, and Wave Speed, p. 95

1. $f = 0.5$ Hz; $T = 2$ s; $\lambda = 6$ m; $v = 3$ m/s

2. $f = 1.6$ Hz; $T = 0.62$ s

3. 5.13×10^3 m/s

4. 3.29×10^{14} Hz

5. 1.6×10^5 m

6. 0.20 Hz

The Electromagnetic Spectrum, p. 96

Region	Wavelength range	Frequency range
radio waves	> 30 cm	$< 1.0 \times 10^9$ Hz
microwaves	30 cm − 1 mm	1.0×10^9 Hz − 3.0×10^{11} Hz
infrared (IR) waves	1 mm − 700 nm	**3.0×10^{11} Hz − 4.3×10^{14} Hz**
visible light	700 nm − 400 nm	**4.3×10^{14} Hz − 7.5×10^{14} Hz**
ultraviolet (UV) light	**400 nm − 60 nm**	7.5×10^{14} Hz − 5.0×10^{15} Hz
X rays	**60 nm − 10^{-4} nm**	5.0×10^{15} Hz − 3.0×10^{21} Hz
gamma rays	0.1 nm − 10^{-5} nm	3.0×10^{18} Hz − 3.0×10^{22} Hz

These regions should be marked between the axes at the bottom of the page to match the ranges in the table, and should be similar to the electromagnetic spectrum diagram in the Background Information.

The Law of Reflection, p. 97

1.

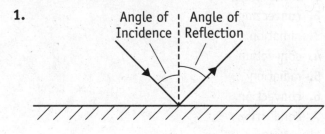

2.

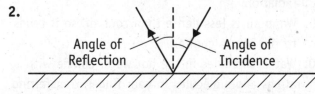

3.

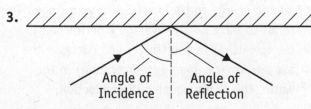

4.

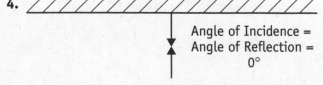

Answer Key
Physical Science, SV 0425-5

ANSWER KEY cont'd.

5.

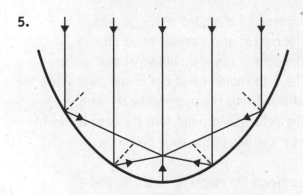

Refraction and Snell's Law, p. 98

1. $\theta_r = 19.2°$

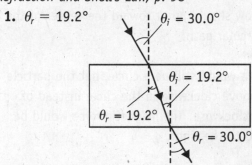

2. A refracted ray should be drawn inside the prism at an angle 19.2° to the right of the normal line. This angle of refraction should be labeled.

3. The refracted ray should be extended to the bottom of the prism.

4. $\theta_r = 30.0°$

5. A normal line should be drawn perpendicular to the surface boundary at the point of incidence. A refracted ray should be drawn outside the prism at an angle 30.0° to the right of the normal line. This angle of refraction should be labeled.

6. The two rays are at the same angle, so they are parallel.

Waves Word Find, p. 99

1. energy	**2.** medium
3. crest	**4.** trough
5. compression	**6.** rarefaction
7. wavelength	**8.** hertz
9. ray	**10.** refraction

```
C R I M X C V H J L Y D O Y R U
G W V Y A R X Z W H A G O I M I
J A N C B L S L G Z J K R P P D
C V U Z R G C Y A L P O U E F H
O E Y B H E Z R K K W C B X N I
M L N B H Q S K W S R Z E M P E
P E H M E G B T Z D V E U N I F
R N B E H M U N D Y H I K E M G
E G F G J L L O Z I D D D Y I D
S T M S M H V K R E J H C T I P
S H X Z E Z W O M T C N Y O T K
I R A R E F A C T I O N V Q M M
O F T N O J L B R R O L F L A K
N Z A W X A Q Q C O F L C X O E
N O I T C A R F E R K O A A D U
R B V W T P Q Q W N T R X C R G
```

Unit 7 — Electricity and Magnetism

Electricity and Magnetism Review, p. 108

1. B	**2.** D
3. C	**4.** B
5. C	**6.** D
7. C	

8. The poles repel one another with a magnetic force.

Electric Charge and Electric Force, p. 109

1. a) 18
  b) 3.2×10^{-19} C

2. a) 2.5×10^{12}
  b) 6.4×10^{-2} N
  c) repulsive

3. a) 8.2×10^{-8} N
  b) 3.6×10^{-47} N
  c) The electric force is much larger.

ANSWER KEY cont'd.

Potential Difference, Current, and Resistance, p. 110
1. 160 Ω
2. 2.4×10^2 V
3. a) 5.0×10^2 V
   b) 1.0×10^3 V
   c) 1.0×10^5 V
4. 5.2 A
5. a) 38 Ω
   b) 5.8 A

Series and Parallel Circuits, p. 111
1. Circuit A is a series circuit; Circuit B is a parallel circuit.
2. 40 Ω
3. 2.9 A
4. 1.6 Ω
5. 72 A
6. 14 A
7. The parallel circuit (B) has the brightest lights.
8. None of the bulbs would light up.
9. All of the bulbs would light up except for the bulb with the broken filament.

Electric Power, p. 112
1. 5.0×10^5 W
2. 4.2×10^{-2} A
3. 118 V
4. 6.50×10^2 V
5. a) 8.00×10^2 W
   b) 6.00×10^2 W
   c) 75.0 W
   d) 1.48×10^3 W
6. a) 115 V
   b) 2.00 A

The Magnetic Field Around a Wire, p. 113
1. The current arrow should point upward.
2. The current arrow should point downward.
3. The field should point out of the page above the wire and into the page below the wire.
4. The field should point into the page above the wire and out of the page below the wire.

Charges Moving in Magnetic Fields, p. 114
1. 4.8×10^{-19} C
2. 7.2×10^{-17} N
3. The arrow should point toward the center of the ion's circular path.
4. 1.6 T
5. The path would still be a circle, but the particle would move clockwise in the circle instead of counterclockwise. The magnetic force would be directed to the right.

Electricity and Magnetism Crossword, p. 115

ACROSS
4. parallel circuit
5. ion
7. watts
8. amperes
9. domain
11. coulombs
12. ohms
13. electron
14. insulator

DOWN
1. magnetic poles
2. electric field
3. alternating current
6. teslas
10. voltage